THE SPIRIT OF
MEDITERRANEAN PLA

MICHEL BUTOR

The Spirit of Mediterranean Places

Translated by Lydia Davis

THE MARLBORO PRESS | NORTHWESTERN
Evanston, Illinois

The Marlboro Press/Northwestern
Northwestern University Press
Evanston, Illinois 60208-4210

Printed in the United States of America

ISBN 0-8101-6052-8

Library of Congress Cataloging-in-Publication Data

Butor, Michel.
    [Génie du lieu. English]
    The spirit of Mediterranean places / Michel Butor ; translated by
Lydia Davis.
        p. cm. — (Marlboro travel)
    ISBN 0-8101-6052-8 (alk. paper)
    1. Butor, Michel—Journeys—Mediterranean Region. 2. Mediter-
ranean Region—Description and travel. I. Davis, Lydia. II. Title. III.
Series.
PQ2603.U73Z477513 1997
848'.91409—dc21   97-29552
                                                                        CIP

CONTENTS

FOUR CITIES   1

   CORDOBA   3
   ISTANBUL   19
   SALONICA   29
   DELPHI   41

A GLIMPSE OF . . .   61

   MALLIA   63
   MANTUA   67
   FERRARA   73

EGYPT   77

The Spirit of
Mediterranean
Places

FOUR CITIES

CORDOVA

for Roland Barthes

And so I must at last talk about Cordova, give an initial and necessarily unsatisfactory form to all those murmurs that continue, that will no doubt continue for years to be roused in me by the name of that city and the memory of my walks or my pauses within its network of white streets, along its sand-colored and whitewashed walls, in the cleanliness of the sun and the coolness of the precise shadows it cast, triangles or trapezoids changing proportions according to the day and the hour, the memory of my patient but too brief efforts to read it, to draw from it the nourishment I was certain of finding in it.

3

I said I would talk about Cordova; now the moment I decided on has come; no more postponements; if I can't settle my debt, I must at least pay something on account; I have to begin to keep the promise that I made not to any human being but inwardly to that city even before I saw it with my own eyes, when I still knew it only from hearsay and through mediocre pictures, already sure, from the figure produced by that collection of precarious information, that here was a place I was bound to visit, a source at which I must inevitably go and drink some day, however polluted its waters might be (what was I to know about that?).

And this promise was all the more forcibly reaffirmed in me the moment I saw that I hadn't been mistaken in my expectations, that the answer this city was giving me, previously unformulable, to the questions I was asking it now was purer, more certain, firmer, more intricate than I could have hoped.

Here I am, then, already talking about Cordova despite my incompetence, just as some day, I don't know when (and for me it will be a much bigger undertaking, attending to it, even temporarily, will call for a great many more pages) I will at last have to talk about my Egypt.

*

I examine all these photographs I brought back from Cordova, the infinitely varied geometry of those streets with their sharp angles, their walls dazzling or mod-

eled by a subtle wear of vegetal inventiveness, with
their rare passersby, silent but not at all lifeless, not at
all abandoned, not presenting anything of that spectacle of broken down men and things so common in
other Andalusian towns, silent because of their civilization, their disdain for noise, because they are steeped
in a tranquil, muted life, in the sort of profound inner
wholesomeness which all of a sudden blossoms in the
middle of a naked wall in a wonderful window framed
with ancient sculptures, or gushing with violet flowers
around a palm branch dating from the preceding Palm
Sunday that with their delicate plaits transform the
mass of light, elsewhere as heavy and compact as an
ingot, into little rivulets, or again, behind the thick
blinds hanging unrolled, those streets animated by the
rustling of a dress, by the life, the intimacy one keeps
glimpsing without disturbing it through those bars of
supple iron, beyond those corridors cooled by their ce-
ramic facings, in the filtered light, in the furniture
standing among the plants, in the magnificent vegetation that now and then emerges from the depths of
those dwellings, transforming a crossroads into a patio,
into a true public living room, calm and restful as
though it were protected not only by a door and a
wall, but by a whole complex of surrounding apartments.

Those streets completely invaded by sleep, by the
regular breathing of sleep, by its quality of persistence,
those streets with names written in black letters as
brilliant and oily as if they had been painted with very

thick printer's ink no sun could ever dry, on the gleaming whiteness, that overabundant whiteness of the glazed tiles,

that cart, that lantern, that fountain, that altar in the middle of the street with its somber paintings behind panes of glass and that superb harmony of dark browns which I reconstruct, those square or octagonal belltowers like minarets, and especially, necessarily, the mosque, which I couldn't help coming back to every day, since it was truly the core of it all, for instance that shadow of a palm tree on an arcade, like a splash, with that child, as though he were caught in a trap, fleeing in a spot of light,

all these photographs are like the index cards a teacher fills in the course of his reading when he intends to talk about a writer, quotations I tried to choose carefully and excise from this large foreign text I was familiarizing myself with and which I translated into my own language.

At this point I will ask for the help, I might almost say intercession, of the poet Luis de Gongora who, finding himself in Granada, wrote this sonnet to the city of his birth, which has changed very little since his time, which had already been sound asleep for a long time, dreaming tranquilly of its ancient empire, fruitfully dwelling upon the enduring glimmers of its splendor, from street to street, from courtyard to courtyard, from wall to wall, from one skin to the next, from one smile or one look to the next, dyeing every new construction with its own color, assimilating imported styles by imposing on them its own love of the rhythmical wall, its obsessive memory of cliff and sand.

A CORDOBA

Oh excelso muro, o torres coronadas
de honor, de majestad, de gallardia!
Oh gran rio, gran rey de Andalucia,
de arenas nobles, ya que non doradas!

Oh fertil llano, oh sierras levantadas,
que privilegia el cielo y dora el dia!
Oh siempre gloriosa patria mia,
tanto por plumas cuanto por espadas!

Si entre aquellas ruinas y despojos
que enriquece Genil y Dauro baña
tu memoria no fué alimento mio,

nunca merezcan mis ausentes ojos
ver tu muro, tus torres y tu rio,
tu llano y sierra, oh patria, oh flor de España!*

---

* Oh high wall, oh towers crowned
   with honor, majesty and valor!
   Oh great river, great king of Andalusia,
   with sands that are noble even though they are
                                    not golden!

7

Only if you have not seen Cordova, have not felt its lofty benevolent sweetness, in communication with everything most enriching that Mediterranean Africa and Islam have to offer us, will you not understand in what sense the memory of it, which occupies a very distinct mental space, can and must be a kind of food. Gongora felt tied to his native land by a private obligation; it was so important to what he was, to the way his mind was formed, that he had to consider it otherwise than as a pure object, and he only attained his highest sincerity in speaking of it when he used the second person. This was no mere "poetic method" derived from some handbook, but really necessary to the kind of special relationship which can only be expressed in this way, which authentically lays the foundations for a process that others may imitate, emptying it of its substance, only because it was first properly invented in this way.

I feel in myself some glimmer of this obligation

Oh fertile plain, oh high sierras,
that privilege the sky and gild the day!
Oh my native land ever glorious
as well for your pens as for your swords!

If among these ruins and spoils
enriched by Genil and bathed by Douro
your memory has not been my food

Let my absent eyes never again deserve
to see your wall, your towers and your river,
your plain and your sierra, oh native land, oh flower
of Spain!

which tied Gongora to Cordova, a very attenuated glimmer, of course, since my stay there was very brief, since I wasn't born in that city, since I was in no way shaped by it, and yet sufficiently manifest, for although I wouldn't have been able to invent those verses (this, apart from any consideration of literary quality) I am nevertheless capable of adopting them, murmuring them on my own.

Of course, when he speaks to us of walls and towers, I think he has in mind a city wall that doesn't really exist any more today, but how could he have separated it from the other, inner city wall that is still intact and the minaret that had just been topped with a Baroque coping? When he speaks to us of swords, he is thinking primarily of the Great Captain, González of Cordova, who must have seemed to his contemporaries as the outstanding glory of his town and whom I don't care much about; when he speaks of pens, the humanist in him was obviously referring to Seneca and Lucan, whom I know only slightly and who take us back to the Roman stage of this city, a stage which for the moment only appears to me as a rather dark sub-basement almost entirely covered by what has fructified on its ruins; but in the 15th century wasn't Cordova known as another Athens? Let's not forget that when he came back from Salamanca, this degree-holder must have known he was returning to the native land of Averroes, the capital of the Caliphs, of which the central organ, the immense mosque containing the very recent cathedral in its very heart, almost camou-

9

flaging it inside its bays, remained, still remains the impressive, the irrecusable evidence.

I can adopt on my own account the reference to Granada, those ruins and those spoils enriched by the Genil and bathed by the Douro: on that heap of marvels, what degradation! In that commotion, what death! A superb carcass, but so far rotted that you risk being overcome by nausea as soon as you leave the preserved areas, a city which is today utterly corrupted by the tourism that reigns there as absolute master, which infects the streets and the children so that one feels one is oneself an agent of that decrepitude, one of the microbes of that disease. Whereas in Cordova, even though I was a tourist there too, I knew very well that my passing through was not polluting those deep waters at all: so strong is the life of the city there that the afflux of visitors only disturbs its surface, this life which has lasted, which has continued, one feels, since the 10th century.

*

Everything, then, always takes us back to the Caliphate, to the time when it was the Byzantium of the West to which Emperor Nicephorus Phocas sent his mosaic-workers with three hundred twenty quintals of little cubes of glass, back to the mosque in which that moment of History is incarnated and endures, so that I can see it, so that from now on it occupies a clearly determined place in my imagination among so many others.

It is the hearth from which all its originality radiates, it is the core so powerfully constituted, the citadel so solidly established that wave after wave of foreigners have failed to make a breach in it, have succeeded only in covering it with new Gothic, Renaissance or Churrigueresque ornaments, as with a vegetation that camouflages it a little but leaves its structure intact; how right it is that it should have the look of a cliff on the outside! This is its safeguard, this form, so powerful that all exterior styles, at least until quite recently, have had to change upon contact with it.

It could not have been destroyed without emptying the city of its pride, its substance. This so obviously, so profoundly Moslem structure had to be Christianized, its very heart stabbed through with a cross like an immobilizing dagger, it had to be branded like a galley slave with this mark to reduce it to obedience, it had to be humiliated, this horizontality, with a vertical choro dominating it through its whole elevation; but the enterprise ended in the most instructive of failures. Not only is the enormous plateresque cathedral swallowed up in the ancient naves like a stone tossed into the middle of a pool and covered by water, so much so that one can walk around it for a long time almost without noticing it; not only does it seem to the spectator like an unfortunate blunder in the middle of that immense canvas, a great blister of tiresomeness, but it pays tribute to what it was supposed to supplant by the very fact that people knew the thing would be possible only if it rivalled the rest in splendor. What is after all admirable about it, the abundantly carved stalls, the sumptuousness of the dark wood, seems to be its contamination by the very enemy it was supposed to vanquish and subjugate, colored the way it is by the shadow of those bays, of those arcades with their infinitely changing and multiplied superimpositions.

Oh, I understand why the monks of Cordova felt such a need to baptise their own church, and why the municipality then became so disturbed about the fact that someone wanted to touch its wonder, destroy, if only in part, that covered space so solidly structured, to which it truly felt its very life and its personality were so closely tied! It was Charles V who decided in favor of the chapter, from a distance, but when he came to see the outcome of the battle for himself, he could only testify to the final defeat of the faction he had supported with those famous words which I can't refrain from quoting too: "If I had known what you wanted to do, you wouldn't have done it, for what you are doing here can be found everywhere and what you had before exists nowhere else."

By now I myself have seen quite a few mosques, in Cairo, Tunisia, and Constantinople, and I can verify that in fact what is here exists nowhere else, that the concept of a building as an orientation of space has never been taken so far.

Let us go into the courtyard which is, like those of all buildings of this kind, a place of public quiet. The fact that the arcades surrounding it have adopted a Gothic ornamentation, which is, moreover, extremely sober, changes nothing; that the minaret has become a bell tower bearing several pilasters, balusters, and obelisks brought from Italy changes nothing; but in order truly to see the great hall, a certain effort of attention and imagination is necessary.

One must reopen all the doors that are walled up now; one must replace those white 18th century vaults by the ceiling of patterned and painted wood of which there remain many scattered pieces and part of which has been reconstructed; one must do away with the plateresque cathedral and everything that disturbs the play of composition of the arcades; finally, one must eliminate all the lanterns that completely distort the distribution of light.

Then one finds oneself in a twilight that darkens as one advances and that vibrates under the trembling flames of the innumerable lamps. If one has come in by the Las Palmas door, one immediately sees the gleaming mihrab, specially lit by its cupola, preceded by the rich crossed arcades of the chapel of Villaviciosa lit in the same way, which, by narrowing the nave, accentuate the impression of distance, and make it seem as though it is situated at the point where those two perfectly rectilinear and parallel colonnades converge.

If one walks forward looking at it, nothing changes, but if one turns one's head in any direction at all, then an immense complexity appears that changes at every step, the double arcs superimposing on one another in all sorts of ways, composing a thousand different figures, creating among themselves illusory relations of proximity that come apart and come back together again every moment, so that one's eyes, after having voluptuously lost themselves in this, are invincibly brought back to the main direction, here not that of Mecca, but southward.

Everywhere else, the interweaving, which is the constant theme of Moslem art, brings the walls to life with fleeting figures that are only there to reduce, to resolve into a multitude of other possible combinations, thus avoiding fixation on idols by drawing every element into an unlimited speech or song; it is only in Cordova, starting with the very first architect, that is, at the end of the 8th century, that we have the achievement of interweaving in space.

The system of double arches is not simply a method of gaining height while avoiding braces, it is the creation of a space multiplied by the projection, on a single row of columns, of the figure given by two rows of simple arches. It is perfectly logical that in the later development of this fundamental theme, such as it is expressed in the richest part of the mosque, Al-Hakim II's expansion, a little column similar to the big one should be applied as an ornament on either side of the pillar separating the spring of the lower arches from that of the higher arches.

With the intersecting and multifoil arches, more and more complex as we approach the mihrab, we see the projection on one and the same plane of figures formed by the superimposition of two rows of double arches; then, in the cupolas whose structure is absolutely original, the use in all three dimensions, above a space which itself has no more need of being oriented, of the combinations thus defined.

One of the doors of the old Aljaferia of Saragossa (11th century), presently in the Madrid archaeology museum, suggests an idea that could have developed this method in amazing ways: two extremely complex multifoil arcades intertwine, and the little ornamental columns, in the midst of this tangle, lean in the direction of their motion as though it were two whole colonnades that were curving in and crisscrossing.

The architectural principle of the Cordova mosque is such that it could have grown almost indefinitely. In fact, the greater the distance from the courtyard to the mihrab, the more accentuated is the sought-after effect of gradual darkening and luminosity by contrast; as for the lateral walls, they are supposed to disappear under the play of superimposed arches, a result which is all the more successful the farther apart they are. Thus, the mihrab was twice pushed back, thus Almanzor had eight bays added on the east side which called for eight more on the west to restore the original symmetry. In some sense the building has an expansive force; it overflows itself. Why should there be anything surprising in the fact that its rich severity, the powerful unity of its growth, its wisdom, continued and still continues to spread through the entire city, despite the vicissitudes of its glory, despite the fall of its empire, despite its diminution, despite its change of religion and culture?

How natural it is that the Inca Garcilaso de la Vega,

bastard son of a conquistador captain and a princess from Cuzco, who remained so profoundly Indian despite the sincerity of his Christianity, should have chosen to be buried in this monument; how natural it is that it should have been in this city, admirable figure of the silent, active endurance of a civilization, that he decided to settle in order to transcribe for us in his masterpiece, the *Royal Commentaries*, the stories he had heard in his childhood.

Gongora certainly knew him and read him, and this affinity, this conjunction enables us to give this line about the Guadalquivir—"sands that are noble even though they are not golden" (which may at first sight seem to be mere padding)—its true resonance. One has to take the word "golden" in its most literal sense, and then one will understand that by this reference to Eldorado, to the fabulous rivers of America which, according to popular rumor, tumbled in their waters enormous nuggets of gold, what he is comparing Cordova to, when he declares that it is just as noble, are the ancient cities of the New World like Cuzco, "that other Rome in its empire," as it was called by the old cross-breed priest who had come from there.

What secret satisfaction must have filled Garcilaso when he walked along the walls of this quadrilateral— they couldn't have failed to remind him of the walls of the fortress whose nooks and crannies he had explored in his childhood games, "whose heights are incredible to anyone who hasn't seen them, and make those who have seen them and looked at them carefully imagine and believe that they were made by magic, and demons and not men made them"—when he entered this still living witness of another conquered civilization, which his Spanish contemporaries were incapable of "replacing by something that achieved the same perfection . . ."

ISTANBUL

I woke up in the train, which was still moving. I lifted the curtain and looked out. I had never in my life seen such desolation. Rain was falling on the Thrace plateau, where not a single tree grew, only small thorny bushes and asphodels among its pebbles. Here and there, inside barbed wire enclosures near their sheet metal camps, Turkish soldiers watched the railway cars go by, coming from the West. We were already several hours late. I closed the curtain and went back to sleep.

The next thing I saw was the long stretch of suburbs on the shores of the Marmara, the airfield and the beaches, then the great golden gate with its two cracked towers of white marble, the maritime ramparts through which we slowly snaked our way, the tall houses of gray wood, the irregular squares, which were not level but littered with rubble, the rising streets, the swarming crowds, the minarets like great pencils.

It was hard getting out of the station. The platform was being repaired, and I had to make my way among piles of stones. The weather had cleared a little.

As soon as I emerged onto the square, I was caught up and deafened by the stridency of the city, by the noise of its taxis and red, yellow or green tramways with their grinding switches, and the large billboards proclaiming the merits of different banks wherever you looked on the black facades of this Oriental Liverpool.

It was lucky for me there was rain and fog the first time I crossed the floating bridge of Galata, which breathes gently under your feet every time a tugboat goes by. This bridge is in fact both a bridge and a railway station with two levels, with many iron stairways, flanked by loading quays with landing steps, for the Bosporus, the Princes Islands or Eyup; with ticket windows, waiting rooms, shops and cafes, congested with a crowd of fishermen dropping their nylon lines, leaning on the railings or crouching on the edges, and with travellers carrying their baskets, or people walking by, dressed in European style, except for their fur caps, but mostly with profoundly foreign faces, with olive skin, wide cheekbones, a slow and uncertain gait.

The coast of Asia was barely visible. Soaked to the skin, worn out because I had been walking for so long, I sat down to drink a glass of tea at a little square green-painted table. In the room, which was decorated only by advertisements in Turkish, other customers were also drinking in silence. Like me, they watched the people walk by, serious in their dark and dull suits, passing between us and the overloaded river buses coming alongside, the small boats in which men were frying freshly-caught fish over a cooker and then stuffing half of each fish into a round loaf, other small boats painted and even sometimes sculpted and hung round with old pieces of tire to cushion the bumps, large caïques with sails, long strings of black barges, to the left the big ships that ran to Smyrna and Alexandria, to the right the cranes, the smoke from the trains, the trees of Gulhane Park, and, above the roofs of the Seraglio with its odd bell tower like a French church, the cupola of Saint Irené, then the Sophia looking as though it were floating, as though it were being borne away in a very slow, imperturbable flight by its four enormous buttresses.

It may be that I never again felt so profoundly the effect of this immense and solemn spectacle, this animated maritime crossroads, this unfolding ceremony, as I did during that disagreeable and Nordic arrival which so amply emphasized the sad and gentle savagery of those ancient nomads who had forgotten their horses amid the wails and whistles of the steamers, the dull tumult of the cars, the knocking of boathooks and oars, the splashing, the cries of the gulls above all this; and yet as I watched it I was delighted by the pearl and amber light that was so wonderfully diffused, re-

21

flected, set in motion by the shimmer of the omnipresent water, I was delighted by all the minarets on the hills like the tent poles of some sumptuous camp, or like reeds in an angel's pool; then, in the evening, everything becoming transfigured in the contagion of the sky's dripping gold, flashing back from that immense luminous horn that plunges into the interior of Europe, dyeing the domes and the depots, dyeing the eyes of men, entering their blood, entering my blood, entering my hands which I no longer recognized as they squeezed the railing which had not only turned to bronze but become the trembling limb of a sleeping wild animal.

Three cities are superimposed on one another, and as one wanders one unravels them, three cities of profoundly different structure, three cities born of three invasions. Let us continue to dwell on the last one, the industrial one, the banking one, the black one, its tramways, its signs, its "tunnel," the underground train that lifts you from Karakoy to Pera, and the Istiklal Caddesi, a long winding thoroughfare, too narrow, overcrowded, with its shops and its bars, that follows the ridge of the hill as far as the immense Taksim square; let us dwell on its traffic lights, its aviation agencies, its bookstores, its restaurants and garages, its effort to make itself secure, to deliver itself from the past, to transform itself and to grow healthier, but let us also dwell on its gummy mud, in which one sinks up to one's ankles on rainy days, its disorder, its gangsters, on the deep feeling of insecurity that it exudes, on its doors barricaded very early in the evening, on the unpleasant loneliness of its streets at night, on the sort of terror that lurks around its gardens and casinos.

This Oriental Liverpool, which grew up so vigorously on the left bank of the Golden Horn, has insinuated itself into old Istanbul on the other side of the river, into the great Ottoman city which has been rotting away for centuries, and it has in some sense put down roots there, suckers in the interstices of its worn and loose fabric, draining its strength. Little by little, concrete buildings, incomparably more solid, are replacing the large houses made of slate-gray wood with their balconies, their innumerable windows set obliquely in relation to the pebbly and gullied street, their little twisted columns, their exterior stairways, their corbels pierced with trefoils, their inscriptions in Arabic characters above the entrance, those old houses that are burning, cracking, eaten by worms, that stand in the midst of kitchen gardens, cemeteries, and wastelands where children run back and forth, pulling on endlessly long strings to raise their kites higher and higher, up into the region of air where another kind of kite, the bird of prey, turns and turns, until suddenly it swoops down on some scrap of refuse.

An encampment that has settled, but without solidifying completely; huts and shanties that have been enlarged and improved, that have been made comfortable, but without ever losing their ephemeral feeling. Turkish Istanbul is a superb abortion, it is truly the expression of an empire that collapsed on itself as soon as it stopped growing. In the great bazaars awning had turned into roof, and especially on the tops of all the hills, raising them even higher, crowning them, finishing them, had been built those great crystallizations, the imperial mosques, and in the lower part of town, their delicate sisters with their facing of faience and their great gray facades. What a city was built during those epochs of grandeur and audacity in the wake of victory, the victory of Mohammed the Conqueror, the victory of Sulayman the Magnificent and his architect Sinan, at the end of the 15th and during the 16th centuries, out of a desire to equal the city in whose ruins it sat! It was more advanced than anything being done in Europe at the time, as we can see from the two splendid groups of buildings named for those two sultans, that of the conqueror having been reconstructed during the 17th century, but more or less on the old plan.

Then, suddenly, the wind went out of the sails. The tradition certainly extended into the beginning of the 17th century with the blue mosque of Ahmet, an attempt was certainly made to revive it in the 18th century with the mosque of Nuri-Osmanieh, and the Tulip Mosque, but these were only isolated efforts, increasingly rare, less and less confident, and the two great islands of order never came together. While the ruins of Constantinople continued to crumble, to subside, earthquakes were already damaging the new buildings.

Let us come now, therefore, to this ghost city, this

city whose rubble we stumble over at every step—with its brick substructures, its ramparts, the large rectangular holes which were once open cisterns, and lastly the churches, which have become sorts of caverns; this city whose very prestige was the cause of its loss—a prestige that remained intact despite its ruin, its diminution; a city which, even while remaining so unknown, since this immense excavation site is still almost entirely unexplored, soon effaces, in the mind of the visitor, almost everything that followed it.

This city was at the origin of everything, it has left its mark on everything. The city itself, we might say, chose this extraordinary site, because it did not come into being as a development of Byzantium, but through the deliberate transferral, to this spot, of the capital of the Roman Empire as it extended into the East. Its huge church, the Hagia Sophia, which is hardly at all denatured by the four minarets that only accentuate its structure, and which reigns incomparable, immediately recognizable, haunted Ottoman architects. After having for a certain length of time prudently avoided imitating an edifice so very expressive of the civilization which they wanted to replace, they found themselves obliged by this irrecusable presence to adapt its structure to their taste, to take it as the basis of their researches, attempting, henceforth, all possible variations in order to tear themselves free of its influence. What are these delicious pools of calm, the mosques of Rustem Pasha or Sokullu Mehmet Pasha, in all their refinement, in all their perfection, compared to the silence that descends on you as soon as you pass under the mosaic of the Virgin between Justinian and Constantine, a humming, gilded silence which has swallowed up in itself the rumbling of thunder, the rustling of leaves in forests, the breaking of waves on shores. The distinction of those slightly broken arcs, all that precise, rational, refreshing elegance, all that good breeding—how much is it worth compared to this magical depth encircling you on all sides and yet fleeing from you? And against this background of splendor, at Fethye Djami or Kharie Djami, we are further humiliated, we are more completely bewitched, by the addition of these figures of grace mysteriously receding in their narrow cupolas.

Little by little the dream assumes a form, when one gathers together all these fragments, when one measures these distances; and above these wastelands, through all these minarets, rises the mirage of Constantinople—the Church of Saint George of Mangana is reconstructed, and once again its gold, as though leaping up from a central spring, flows over its entire surface, as in the description left us by Psellus; once again, it is surrounded by arcades, horses, fields, canals, basins, groves and pools; Sulayman's throne sits once again in the palace of the Magnaure; the Chalcé is covered once again with its bronze tiles, the cisterns fill with water, the hills recover their terraces and their steps—the mirage of this city which from its very beginning was threatened by everything that came from the plateaus, from the interior of the continents, this city which had already been living such a very long time in its own ruins when the breach was made in its walls, this city which safeguarded with such great difficulty a few caverns of the old amber in the midst of the deserted quarters, in the midst of the immense, abandoned, crumbling palaces, this city, more and more solitary, which has itself become the Empire.

The Galata bridge breathes under my feet; I haven't left it. Night is falling. I watch the cranes and the railway cars, I watch the fog coming from Asia, I watch the lights floating on the strait, where the *Argo* still sails, this teeming strait so full of splendor, joy, and apprehension.

SALONICA

There was the water I walked along every day to go to the Lycée Français, shallow water, usually still, covered with patches of gasoline, and, especially when a rather warm breeze blew towards the city, full of a very great number of jellyfish, most of them tiny, bluish and transparent, gently palpitating in their slow and hazardous progress, sometimes enormous, orange and dead.

There was the water, and in the water the big bags of oysters that were put there to cool in front of the entrance to the Olympos-Naoussa Restaurant; and on the other side of the water, most often, was the foggy, dismal horizon of the sea, animated only by little boats with copper-colored striped sails, for, in that roads choked from year to year by the alluvial deposits of the Vardar River, the port was slowly suffocating.

From time to time, the long gray mass of an American warship stopped in the distance. First it would put ashore its police, and you would see them two by two in the streets, with their billies, then it was the sailors themselves in white uniforms.

There was the water, but sometimes it happened that on the other side of the water the immense melody of Mount Olympus would appear, and then you had to go up the green rock steps to see it gradually rise with you, always higher than you, taking on its dimensions and its distance.

For days, for weeks even, it would remain entirely invisible, hidden in the murky light; you would almost forget it, or rather you would begin to doubt your own memories, you would no longer be able to believe in that size, that precision, you would reduce it to more reasonable proportions, more in conformance with its present disappearance, and then abruptly, the next day, it would assert itself again, each time just as surprising, always unexpected.

For this to happen, the atmospheric pressure on the roads would have to be very low, and as a consequence, it was a sign that bad weather was coming. It generally happened at the time when the great freezing wind from Yugoslavia began to blow, raising, in the large straight arteries exactly parallel to it (as though the town planner, apparently a Frenchman, who drew up the plan for rebuilding the city after the big fire of 1917, had wanted to help it lash out) blinding whirlwinds of dust; it was generally during the morning of a winter day that was going to be inclement, that the first rays of the sun, before they reached us through the menacing clouds, illuminated for us those snows and those storm clouds beyond which began a bright country of islands and olive trees, very different from the Balkan land where we were, a country that attracted us just as it had attracted the barbarians, Philip of Macedon, the Dorians, or the first Greeks.

And so there was the water, and along the water the broad quay on which, every evening in good weather, I saw the Greeks taking walks up and down from the port to the white tower, this quay bordered by reinforced concrete buildings which were sometimes painted in delicate colors, built without any sense of proportion or intelligence, then Aristotle Square, in the middle, bordered by arcades in a cut-rate Byzantine style, unfinished, with the store for the English Austin cars, rising streets intersecting at right angles other long parallel streets swept by violent gusts. This was the new city, stretching along the roads indefinitely in suburbs of bourgeois villas and shacks for the refugees who had come from Anatolia in 1923.

Above, there was the old city with an immense no-man's-land in the middle of it, sloping, with permanent little merry-go-rounds of rudimentary airplanes or cars for children, and a great number of green-painted buses (which looked as though they were not in service, but which actually provided regular service on all the province's main routes), with its churches generally below the level of the street, and naturally the more sunken the older they were, with the cupolas of its Turkish baths, with its unused mosques and the bases of its fallen minarets, with its beautiful timbered houses that were being gradually razed, with its crooked little streets, with its stairways and the green rock that appeared more and more often as one went up, like bones poking through the skin or the meat in a butchershop window, with its fountains and its streams, with its sarcophagi unearthed here and there, which have stayed where they are because there is nothing to be done with them, and which are sometimes used as watering-troughs, with the battlements of the ramparts.

And on the other side of this city wall, there was another slope, almost vacant, that they were trying to fill with one-room brick hovels with a single door and a single window, and at the very top the fortress of seven towers, which one couldn't go into because it was the city prison. Finally, the last horizon, when I looked east out my window, were the two peaks of Mount Kortiatys, between which, in the spring, in that disturbing hollow, I would see the morning sun appear as a point of light, then fill out and break free into the sky.

I often walked around the outside of the ramparts. Going through a neighborhood of shopkeepers and warehouses, I would reach Vardar Square, a sad traffic circle above which, in the evening, an illuminated advertisement for a brand of aspirin went on and off obsessively.

I had to take a little oblique street and this began to

my right; first there were formless vestiges, masses of bricks swallowed up in buildings, then the battlements would appear, and the towers; now the houses grew smaller, leaning up against that great wall—shops of shoemakers, tailors and mechanics, dirty little cafes where people drank ouzo and where, sometimes, one could hear people playing the lute and singing Turkish music—against that great wall which went off in zig-zags, scaling the spurs of rock, going down into the steep valleys and back up the other side even higher, with here and there a gate or enormous gaps, here and there superb blocks of white marble engraved with Roman inscriptions, the houses more and more like cankers, like sickly growths on that noble wall, minuscule, miserable shanties with sheet metal roofs.

Then, when I reached the height of the Acropolis, the ramparts stood absolutely bare, the ultimate limit, and there wasn't even any road going around them anymore. I would have to cut across the fields; but these weren't fields, this was the other side, the green desert that began to unroll without habitations, without crops, without trees, with just one or two paths winding through that immensity that one felt stretching out with its stubbly grass, in its monotony, in its dereliction, a desert interrupted only by a few skimpy villages, disorderly and desolate, far from one another, fold after fold all the way to the other mountains, to the borders of Bulgaria peopled, in the city's imagination, with the eyes of innumerable spies.

One day, the snow fell for a long time on Salonica,

and the next day, inside the city walls, the sun made all the roofs sparkle, the dazzling whiteness sharpened all the colors in the streets, which had suddenly become wonderfully clean; I was accompanied by the bright song of dripping water coming from all sides. But outside, as though even stranger and more hostile, I saw that frozen expanse with its glinting pools and big wet patches. Then I felt more exiled than ever before. This was no longer Europe then; for me, the capital of Macedonia became like the city of Merv in Turkmenistan, and among the workers who were approaching in a group, who loomed up against the indeterminate distance, I was quite prepared to recognize the abominable veiled prophet whose adventure is told to us by Borges in his universal history of infamy. Then as if by a very distant memory I was invaded by the insecurity, the unfocused fear that is aroused in us by the word "barbarism" with its menacing significance acquired at the time of the Empire's decline.

Others will say it was merely the stifling heat of summer.

*

Certainly, Athens has more attractions, with the purity of its air, with its marble monuments, with its gardens, with the wonderful abrupt elegance of its hills, with its special situation surrounded by the most sublime ancient sites conveniently visited using it as a departure point or a home base, with its museums, with its big-city comforts and entertainments. But if I still have a special attachment to Salonica, it is not only because I spent much more time there; it is because at every step in the streets which are today laid over the site of the illustrious queen of theater, the ridiculous neo-classical buildings of the 19th century (one wonders how it is possible that having impressive fragments of the most perfect originals constantly before their eyes, this new population could have been, and still is, satisfied with such crude imitations), at every step these evidences of a Greece totally imported from England, from France or from Germany—a Greece designed, or I would almost say determined, by what was most reactionary, most closed, least in touch with the ancient creative energy in Western societies of that time, a Greece which all of recent research shows us to be, as was certainly obvious, a total misconception of Greece—these buildings intolerable because of their pretentious vulgarity force on us the feeling of a profound historic discontinuity. However touching and manifestly admirable the few vestiges of the works of Phidias or Ictinus that have survived into our time. I am all too aware of the systematic and scandalous use made of them in this country, not to feel a great distrust of those who tell me they are superior to everything else, which they can't be anyway, and not to forgive the young Greeks who refuse to hear about them.

At the beginning of the 19th century, before the war of independence, there was nothing at the base of the most famous acropolis of all but an infinitesimal village, and the capital that has grown up around it, although it certainly lies on the same ground as the ancient city, is in no sense an extension of it, but something completely different, a modern Mediterranean city which has no more relation to it than the Alexandria of today has to that of the Ptolemies, a city which, while having in its heart the most precious of ruins, has shown, at least up to the past few years, that it is incapable of drawing from them any authentic advantage whatever for its present-day architecture.

In Salonica, on the contrary, in Salonica the dull, the foggy, the dusty, the muddy, the provincial, in Salonica so distant from every important ancient site, what awaits the attentive and patient traveller, through all the decay, is the density of a city that has not ceased to be a city and a border city from the time it was founded some years after the death of Alexander. It is the very last wave come from Byzantium that expires here at our feet, under the tide of an inevitable and disorderly Westernization.

While it is not, properly speaking, a part of Greece, Salonica, halfway between Athens and Constantinople (still considered by most of the population to be the true capital, now lost, the other being merely a makeshift), is of all places the best to experience that amazingly misunderstood but obvious fact, that from the dazzling civilization of Greece up to our time there is not only the road that leads through Rome and the Italian Renaissance, but also, intersecting it more often than one would imagine, the road marked out by the monuments of the Empire and the Eastern Church.

Under the citadel of Theseus, from Ceramicus to Lycabettus, there are of course a few small medieval churches, but however charming their exteriors may be, mere shells whose internal decoration has always disappeared, they only rarely succeed in arousing the visitor's interest, squeezed as they are between the brilliant pagan ruins and the buildings of today. In Salonica, not only does there remain a group of related monuments, incomparably more spread out in time, incomparably more important and significant despite their deplorable condition today, but also, around them, traces of the urban organization of which they were the ultimate flowering, the focal points.

But it is important to remember that among all the ancient worlds, the one we call Byzantium is one of those of which the fewest pieces of evidence have survived, and we would risk the most undertandable sort of disappointment if we approached these poorly patched together remnants—Saint George, Saint Demetrius or the Holy Apostles—in their decrepitude without having in our memory images from other places that allow us to complete them, to reconstruct their youth.

*

Today, I want to celebrate just one of them, the one that has nourished me, comforted me the most of all of them, the mosaic of the apse in the church of Hosios David which is almost all that is left of the Monastery of the Quarryman, dating from the last years of the 5th century, that is, a little after the mausoleum of Galla Placidia at Ravenna, before San Vitale, disfigured by many cracks painted over with that horrible pommade pink so fiercely beloved of the often pitiful representatives of the present-day Orthodox clergy.

All I will describe is its subject. The center is inspired by a passage from the Apocalypse: a young Christ with a halo sits on a rainbow in the middle of a transparent, nacreous circle (the abundance of silver was one of the most remarkable characteristics of the mosaics of that period in Salonica); but whereas the apostle says: "I saw in the right hand of The One sitting on the throne a scroll, sealed with seven seals," the Savior of Hosios David has his right hand raised, and it is in his left hand that he holds unrolled a volume on which is inscribed, not the seven famous maledictions, but a prayer that can be roughly translated as: "Take care, oh our God, in whom we place our hope, and thanks to whom we rejoice in our salvation, to bring peace to this house." Around him fly the angel, the eagle, the bull and the lion, all holding the bound books of their gospels, their two great wings spangled with eyes, like the tails of the peacocks that ornament the gold structures in the cupola of Saint George, or of those live ones that walk in the gardens of another monastery under the ramparts.

Saint John attributes six to each of them, and the

source of this whole part of his vision is another Biblical vision: "And I looked, and, behold, a whirlwind came out of the north, a great cloud, and a fire infolding itself, and a brightness was about it . . . Out of the midst thereof came the likeness of four living creatures . . . they had the likeness of a man. As for the likeness of their faces, they four had the face of a man, and the face of a lion, on the right side; and they four had the face of an ox on the left side; they four also had the face of an eagle . . . behold one wheel upon the earth by the living creatures, with his four faces . . . and their rings were full of eyes round about them four. And above the firmament that was over their heads was the likeness of a throne, as the appearance of a stone: a sapphire and upon the likeness of the throne was the likeness as the appearance of a man above upon it . . . and it had brightness round about. As the appearance of the bow that is in the cloud on the day of rain . . ." introducing the book of Ezekiel.

He is the one in the left corner, standing on ground that is hilly and as though dislocated by a tremor, he is doubled over in an attitude of terror and reverence, his two hands raised against his temples. But on the other side, another prophet, Habakkuk, in a completely different attitude, sitting, his hand on his chin, ponders, doubts God's justice. It is no longer God's appearing that frightens him, but His absence, his equanimity restored only when God's power at last seems to manifest itself:

With torrents you split the earth;
The mountains see you, they tremble;
A cloudburst passes,
The abyss makes its voice heard,
It reaches up its hands.

And we see it, that abyss, we see it howl, actually lift its hands, in the form of an old man of silver who emerges from one of the four rivers coming together at the Savior's feet.

Lastly, the big city that is depicted behind Ezekiel is Babylon, one source or at least one resurgence of the liquor that flowed in part for me, flowed through distillations and negations of all sorts, after so many adventures and new beginnings, the liquor I drank my fill of, seeping from the porous curved wall in a gentle trickling of light at the end of a deserted alleyway in Salonica.

DELPHI

1. THE SITE

Since I too was coming from Crete, my mind still full
of the Minoan paintings, it obviously would have been
better to make the crossing by sea and land at the port
of Itea, near the ancient city of Crissa that was destroyed by direct order of the god, who brought certain
sailors here by force, taking the shape of an enormous
dolphin and leaping aboard their ship in the middle of
the sea as they were coming from Knossos, diverting
them from their route so that they could become the
celebrants of his cult in the mountaian—and after
landing, it would have been better to climb up, like
them, through the woods to the sanctuary.

But because it was early January, I had to come from

Athens by bus through Thebes and Levadhia, in the rain, during the shortened winter afternoon, all the way to that crepuscular, windswept road where, as I might have expected, I found that all the places with restaurants and heat mentioned in my blue guide, the traveller's precarious support, were closed.

The owners of the only functioning *estiatorion* had not anticipated that another voracious foreign mouth would be coming to share their meager supper, and so the only door that opened to welcome me was the door of the Hotel Parnassus, where I slept chilled to the bone despite the six blankets, at least, that had been given me in a terribly cold and very clean room whose window looked out over the roofs of the houses across the way onto the immensity of the landscape and the darker and darker sky that was clearing, revealing its stars little by little above a sea whose presence was felt in the indentation of the steep slope, and leaving a few patches of fog here and there.

In the morning, as the sun rose over the great field of terraced white boulders which are the ruins of the Apollonian kingdom, through the by now magnificently clear air and sky, and moved to the south, its rays, reflected by the two "diamonds," vertiginous, granular mirrors of rocks whose focal point seems to be the temple itself, were striking, burning harder and harder, a sweet deflagration of arrows, so that in the very heart of this highland winter, which I had felt to be so penetrating all night long despite the latitude, the summer in all its force was given back to me inside this

gigantic open hearth, suspended midway to the sky
above a dark ravine so vertical and so densely wooded
that one can't even see to its bottom, from which one
hears the sound of Pleistos's rumbling rise up; inside
this divine theater of which the theater that still has its
marble tiers is only a minuscule adaptation on human
scale; inside this oven that concentrates not only heat,
not only the light of the day to the point where it is as
though one has entered the explosion of a stable kind
of lightning, but also sound, also our speech, which is
magnified here until it seems to have the dimensions of
thunder, so much so that it appeared to me that if the
words of an ode were chanted here they would necessarily be propagated across these gorges, thrown from
one echo to the next, from one wave to the next, over
the sea that comes into view deep in the distance at a
turn in the road, as far as Sicily, an impression that is
indissociable in my memory from the beginning of the
first *Pythian Ode* where Pindar, whose iron seat was
kept in the temple itself and who is the poet par excellence of Delphi, declares, in praise of his art, that "all
that Zeus does not love trembles, hearing the song of
the Pierides, feared on the earth and on the sea, especially he who lies in frightful Tartarus, the enemy of
the gods, hundred-headed Typhon" crushed under the
mass of Etna, arousing its volcanic fury; and we must
try for an equivalent of his style in our own language,
inventing and manipulating rhythmic and grammatical
structures as ample and strong as his "long solemn
strophes" and his supple sentences enjambing them, in

order to attempt to give this place praise worthy of it.

Because what is important above all else here is the place. Because here as everywhere else, more than anywhere else, perhaps, in this Greece where so few ancient monuments are still standing, but where so many ancient remains are still buried, seeds of knowledge that germinate under the pick of the digger, that flower so slowly under our gaze, we must come and question the site itself. Because it was already a temple, made special by its very configuration, before the time of all these constructions, whose plan is sketched on the stepped rocks by rows of stones in the midst of a few trees and a little grass, and whose elevation I sought to imagine, those shelters of stone hung with shields and swords, a profusion of all sorts of votive offerings crowded against one another, embedded in one another, covering one another, all painted with the most vivid colors wherever they couldn't be gilded, with a crowd of statues, and the consciousness of this antecedence was expressed by the presence just in front, just beneath the sub-basement of the large temple, of the area of ground that remained bare in the midst of the savannah of monuments, the sanctuary of Gaea, the earth.

2. THE TEMPLE

Around the god's enclosure, especially down below, there remain some traces of the greedy little town with its hotels and displays of religious objects, which people say became another Lourdes, or even worse, very cynically and systematically exploiting the public's credulity, degrading more and more a cult that had been maintained artificially for centuries, starting from the time they completed Apollo's last sanctuary, of which the worn shafts of six columns have now been put back up; starting when, Philip of Macedon being the ruler of Greece, the essential role the oracle had played in the Hellenic world as the equilibrator of the cities began to weaken irreversibly; but we would fail to understand anything about Delphi and indeed anything about the entire civilization of ancient Greece if we imagined that the pythia amounted at that time to mere fraud, if we failed to look beyond that enormous cloud of venal charlatanism and rediscover the brightness that caused the eyes of Michelangelo's Sibyl to open in such wonder and whose glimmer Nerval could still see, the authenticity of the oracle, that "national exegete," as Plato called it, the instrument whereby Greek society—whose unity, despite all its internal feuds and wars, despite its extreme fragmentation, was periodically reaffirmed in the gatherings at the four great games, the Olympic, the Pythic, the Isthmic and the Nemean—became capable of clarifying and objectifying its fears, its propensities, the beliefs it shared in opposition to the rulings of this or that state or particular group of states, an organ so essential that this society considered it to be the center of its universe, the "omphalos," the navel or hub, what unified its different parts,

this last temple, one of whose pediments depicted

the Delian triad, Leto with her twin bow-carrying children, Apollo and Artemis, surrounded by muses with
the sunset, and the other Dionysus among his dancing
priestesses, the Thyiades; this temple in the interior of
which one could see first the inscriptions of the Seven
Sages, Homer's statue, and a mysterious epsilon; then,
in the central room, which was already very dark compared to the dazzling exterior though lit by a perpetual
fire, an altar to Poseidon, the statues of the Parcae or
Moirae, and the statue of Apollo ruling them, com-
manding them, leading them, the "expounders of
Fate," and Pindar's iron seat,

down below, the waiting room for the people con-
sulting the oracle, where the darkness was even
thicker, filled with sulfurous vapors which have dried
up by now, but which must have mingled with many
different sorts of fumes and made the air almost un-
breathable in the "adytum," the holy of holies, a cav-
ern lit only by the glow of the torches or oil lamps that
awoke, in the midst of the acrid drifting cloud, a few
gleaming points on the gilding and the nacreous eyes
of the idol of Apollo "loxias," the oblique, the
enigmatic, beside Dionysus's sarcophagus and the
large conical stone that has been preserved for us, the
navel itself, the tomb of Python, in those days completely swathed in wrappings, the delirium-producing
exhalations issuing from the lips, closed now, of Gaea
the inspirer, from that cleft over which an ignorant old
woman mumbled on her tripod,

this last temple that replaced the one the great tra-

gedians knew, of which the two very mutilated pediments have been recovered: on one side the Delian
triad, Leto, Artemis, and Apollo, on a chariot pulled by
four horses, surrounded by young men and women
between two groups of fighting animals, and on the
other, the giants defeated by the Olympians under the
leadership of Athena,

of which there remains on the site the magnificent
supporting wall of great blocks of golden white marble, cut as though to imitate enormous fish-scales, irregular polygons with rounded corners, covered with
inscriptions engraved in meticulous, minuscule characters, and so precisely fitted together that even today
scarcely a blade of grass manages to take root in their
interstices, which is why it was able to withstand the
earthquake of 373 B.C., which toppled the whole
structure it supported, and all the earthquakes that
followed,

the temple built at the instigation of a great family
exiled from Athens, the Alcmenides, thanks to offerings which came not only from all the properly Hellenic islands and cities, but also from Croesus, King of
Lydia, and from the Pharaoh Amasis,

to replace the temple founded, according to legend,
by two architects who had come from Orchomenus,
Agamedes and Trophonius, and destroyed by a fire in
548,

a temple which, so Pausanias, author of a "blue
guide" to Greece for pious tourists of the second century A.D., was told nearly seven hundred years after

47

the fact (certainly many traditions had had time to be lost or corrupted) itself replaced three other temples:

the one described in a few lines of a paean by Pindar, most of which has been lost: "of bronze were the walls, of bronze also the standing columns, and above the ridge sang six gilded sorceresses," that was said to have been built, cast, by Hephaestus and that was hurled into an abyss by a bolt of lightning,

the one of wax and transparent wings built earlier by bees, which was obscurely related to Crete and was said to have been carried off by Apollo to the Hyperboreans,

and, finally, the earliest of them all, a hut formed of laurel branches brought from the Vale of Tempe.

3. APOLLO

As the Hellenic civilization broke up into clearly defined kingdoms and especially into republics that were more and more jealous of their own peculiar organizations, gods who had at first been common to almost the entire area of Greece, whether they were of Aegean background, of Asiatic influence, or had been brought by one of the waves of invasion, acquired a distinct history and signification in each of their places of worship, according to its characteristics, but since this differentiation took place within a community that subsisted not only by means of a constant retail trade but also through the ritual expression of this trade in the regular encounters of the great games, these myths, more and more divergent from one another, would come face to face, and one of the main duties of the poets was to strain their wits to resolve the myths' differences by reuniting their episodes into one common legend, and this was indispensable to the safeguarding of their language since the names of the gods obviously appeared to be the most important words and a way had to be found to make these names continue to designate identical realities, but it was also something that caused a profound transformation, since there was only one way to link these juxtaposed stories, these acts attributed in different places to one and the same god in independent liturgical sequences: and this was to try to interpret them in the light of individual human motives, so that the relations among the themes became more and more psychological, at the same time as the themes became more and more detached from the ritual, and fable was gradually substituted for the ancient myths.

In this way, the Homeric hymn to Apollo, at least in the form in which it has been handed down to us (for most of the experts agree in recognizing not only two traditions here, but also two authors) tries to stitch together the two autonomous legends that had developed in the two most famous sanctuaries of the god, the legend of Delos and the legend of Delphi.

The latter tells us that he came accompanied by muses from Pieria, that is, from the Vale of Tempe in Thessaly which was the source, Pausanias was told, of

49

the laurel branches forming the most ancient of his temples, and whence a new branch was brought back every eight years by the leader of the procession, the architheoros, on the occasion of the feast of Septeria commemorating his taking possession of the place;

then he built the foundations on which Agamedes, of whom we know almost nothing, and Trophonion, the ancient god of the Mynians, a people who came from Thessaly to Orchomenus, a hero in one place and an oracle in another, laid down a threshold of stone "around which the numberless families of the men raised a temple of hewn stone in order that it be forever worthy of song";

and as he was wondering who would attend to his cult, he saw a ship on the sea coming from the Minoan Knossos and he leapt onto its deck, taking the form of a dolphin (whence his surname, Delphinios, and also the name of Delphi itself), forcing them to change course and land at the port of Crissa, where he revealed himself to them in the form of a youth, explained what he expected of them, ordered them to accompany him, singing the Cretan paean, while he walked up to his sanctuary sounding his lyre.

It was before Thebes was founded by the Phoenician Cadmus, and at a time when these regions, now so denuded for the most part, were covered with forests, at the height of the Mycenaean era, that different rituals began to come together and fuse in the crucible of Parnassus, rituals that had come from Thessaly by way of Orchomenus, and from Crete, and no doubt from many other regions, and that were already very different, but all addressed to the same god, Apollo, of whom certain essential characteristics, a common core that he had preserved through his navigations and adventures, was in such admirable harmony with this new dwelling that it gave them, it gave him, an increased manifestness, an increased power.

Phoebus, the dazzling one, he arrives in this solar oven, involved with the laurel in a laurel wood that has now disappeared, master singer in this natural theater, the new god, a god who bursts in, who imposes himself, suddenly appearing in Olympus and forcing all the other gods to acknowledge him, in what has already been a very venerated sanctuary and even an oracle for a long time.

His victory was so complete and seemed so justified that when Aeschylus, at the beginning of the *Eumenides*, has the pythia invoke the ancient divinities of Delphi, he has her say that the one who came before her there, after Gaea the earth, after Themis who was divine justice, was Phoebe, a Titaness said to be Leto's mother, and that she gave her this place as a gift at the time of the joyous birth.

And so, once he was established there, he showed himself to be the legitimate owner of the place, so well secured in the countryside that for centuries he would be able to stand fast before the new waves of invaders. But if his aspect as soothsayer is so carefully promoted here, it is certainly because there was a conflict, because a new distribution was substituted for the old distribution of temples and divine kingdoms, because an old power was murdered, there was a violent suppression, or rather a conquest and a recovery, the submersion not only of an old cult but of something the cult was a necessary part of, the old arrangement of men and things.

The prophetic voice rises over the sarcophagi of the fallen gods, and if this site was already an oracle before Apollo's triumph, it was no doubt because a supplanting had already taken place there.

4. PYTHON

Now we have come to the heart of the Delphic logos, the primordial fight during which the new young god, the master archer, struck with one of his irresistible arrows the guardian serpent, who began thrashing about on the ground with loud death rattles and "after a prodigious, unspeakable clamor" died in the middle of the forest. Then Phoebus Apollo said to him proudly:

"Now rot here on this earth, which is the mother of men . . ."

And the shadows darkened the beast's eye and the sacred heat of the sun caused him to rot in the very place that was thenceforth called Pytho, meaning rot.

Of course the old gods venerated up to this time did not allow themselves to be thus dispossessed of their territory and their worshippers without resisting;

though defeated, they did not disappear completely; what remains of them is a cadaver that sinks into people's minds and rots, causing nightmares, terrifying mental disturbances.

With this murder, Euripides tells us in one of the choruses of *Iphigenia in Tauris*, Apollo drove Themis from the site of the oracle; he overturned the old religious order; and as revenge for her daughter's humiliation, the earth Gaea gave birth during the night to phantoms that visited multitudes of sleepers and announced, in the greastest confusion, not only what was going to happen, but what had already happened.

But he was able to bring this disorder under control; he persuaded Zeus, one of whose wives Themis became, to do away with the nocturnal voices and the fits of madness. Through his priests, he was able to explain the chaos of images, to interpret this particular instance of the general rottenness, the rottenness of language that was the mumbling of the pythia, a quite localized disorder in which all the dangerous fermentation would finally concentrate, the spoken, public equivalent of the ink spots we interpret under the gaze of the psychologist, projecting onto them, unawares, our contradictions, obsessions, and the ideas operating in us that our everyday consciousness so often has no knowledge of; projecting, there, the religious contradictions, the tangles of the entire complex Hellenic world that they represented as a community, the priests read the present or potential wrath of the gods; they give substance to a disturbance that is felt or feared, and they decide by what means to pacify it, purify themselves.

He is Loxias, that is to say the oblique, the enigmatic, the one through whom the enigma assumes a form, instead of remaining unbounded, pestiferous, destructive.

5. THE BEES

The ancient goddess who was supplanted sinks down into the earth; it isn't necessarily that she was originally chthonic, she became so at the moment she was dispossessed (just as the Olympians and Apollo himself became demons after the Christian submersion).

Now she is a serpent, a dragon, or if she manages to survive, to keep her name and a cult of honor, now she creates serpents and dragons as expressions of her fury, of her defeat; for example, since Zeus had given birth to Athena without her help, Hera herself produced hundred-headed Typhon, as the Homeric hymn to Apollo tells us at length, appearing to abandon its subject suddenly just as it is getting to the main point, the great scene of the fight, but this is not really a digression at all, since for the author, this Typhon, or its double, Typhoeus, had exactly the same signification as Python himself, so that everything that concerned the one had to be able to explain the other, a relationship that throws new light for us on the opening to the first *Pythian Ode* I quoted from earlier, which begins to reveal to us that for Pindar, any execution of an ode to Delphi, insofar as the music makes the monster tremble again, is a reactualization of the murder that was essential to the history of the place.

Python is the massive expression of the fury of these powerful dispossessed goddesses once benevolent, now terrifying, and who have become the very image of divine vengeance, these Parcae or Moirae whom Apollo succeeded in subduing, in binding, and who in Aeschylus's *Eumenides* appear to be defending an ancient right, an ancient concept of kinship relations, in which the child was primarily the son of his mother, and which contrasts with the concept their successor championed, expressed in mythology by the theme of the engendering of Athena by Zeus without the help of Hera:

"The mother is not the one who gives birth to the creature who is called her child; she is only the nurse of the seed planted in her. The one who gives birth is the man who fertilizes her; like a stranger, she safeguards the young shoot."

Which is an answer to the words of the Furies:

"It is the blood of his mother, the blood that flows in his own veins, that he has spilled on the ground."

The pythia is all the more terrorized when she enters the adytum and sees them, horrible, all crouching around suppliant Orestes, because she was once closely tied to these ancient goddesses whom she can no longer recognize in their frightful metamorphosis.

She is constantly being called a bee, her mumbling a kind of buzzing, and in the Homeric hymn to Hermes, we see Python's conqueror, the great decipherer, send away the god of thieves who will soon become the god of writers, because he asked him, in exchange for the gift of the lyre he had just invented, to share with him the privilege of divination; send him back to the three Moirae, the three Venerables, the "virgin sisters proud of their rapid wings, from which a shining powder sprinkles over their heads, who were his teachers in the art of soothsaying ... who remain at the feet of Parnassus whence they take flight to go off in every direction coating themselves with wax ... and who consent to reveal the truth when they are stuffed with honey," back to these bees who have been transformed by his coming, by his victory, into serpents.

Now the cicerones of Delphi assured Pausanias that on the site of the temple he saw, whose remains we are considering, there had been another built by bees, one that Apollo himself had taken into the mysterious country that was his ultimate mythological origin, the country of the Hyperboreans. In this way, he to some extent made up for the perturbation he had caused in the economy of the world of the gods, in the distribution of lands and roles; he made reparation for the insult he had caused to Themis.

6. HEPHAESTUS

As for the other temples which, they told him, had preceded that of Agamedes and Trophonius, it is impossible not to compare the first, the hut made of branches, to the other hut "in the shape of a royal palace," Python's dwelling which is reconstructed every eight years at the time of the festival of the Septeria, that is, the commemoration of Apollo's victory and his establishment at Delphi, after he razed it and burned it. And if at that period it was considered to be already dedicated to Apollo, it was because from a distance all those constructions and destructions eventually resembled one another in view of the importance of the fight, which was essential to the logos of the place, so that as it was being built every temple was considered to belong to the founder, Apollo, whereas when it collapsed it was considered to belong to the serpent.

Without this, wouldn't it be strange and scandalous that the bronze temple, if it was really the rightful property of the dazzling god, should have been hurled into an abyss by a bolt of lightning? Everything becomes clear when legend presents this to us as the work of Hephaestus, who plays a role in Delphi that is half concealed, since he has no stature there, but is also fundamental, since, as the pythia reminds us in Aeschylus, it was his children who opened the road thither for Apollo, "taming the wild ground for him"; Hephaestus whom the Greeks themselves considered to be one of the most obviously prehellenic of all their gods, who is happiest among the inhabitants of Lemnos with their almost unintelligible speech; who is closely connected to the state of things that preceded the one defended by Phoebus, closely connected to the supremely maternal conception of filiation, since he was engendered by Hera "without a love union, in anger and defiance of her husband"; the limping god, humbled like the metal-workers whose patron he is; he to whom, as to Typhon, was assigned as dwelling place henceforth the inside and the base of Mount Etna.

"Of bronze were the walls, of bronze also the columns which stood there," says Pindar, and this insistence on the word bronze is directly reminiscent of the following passage from Hesiod (the resemblance is even more obvious in the original texts): "of bronze were their weapons, of bronze also their houses; with bronze they worked the fields, for black iron did not exist."

He is the god of the bronze age (inevitably we are reminded here of the collection of massive ingots on display in the museum in Crete), the god of the "terrible and powerful" third race that preceded the first iron age, in the age of the Achaean heroes, of the Trojan War and then the Seven Against Thebes, the age we call the Mycenaean, during which Apollo came, the age which, Hesiod tells us, still continues among the blissful Hyperboreans.

7. DIONYSUS

For these mysterious Hyperboreans, in their inaccessible region beyond the north, are the idealized persistence, in the remoteness of space, of a state of things that is gradually disappearing, here, into the remote past; so that when Apollo goes off to stay with them in the autumn, he isn't going back to his geo-

graphical origin, but rather toward the time of his ir-
ruption into Dephi,

ceding his place to the dead god whose sarcophagus
he was guarding and who came back to life every year
in autumn,

ceding his place to Dionysus whose diffusion
throughout Greece was, as we have said, a recurrence
of the past, which here took on a very precise meaning
(just as Euripides tells us that the serpent Python was
the color of wine, and that the summit of Parnassus at
the time when Apollo came was already alive with bac-
chanalian dances),

to Dionysus because he was "the pure light of autumn," and because it was in the spring and summer
especially, in the seasons when the sun's course was
the widest, that the site of Delphi functioned as a solar
oven, so that it was clearly the home of the dazzling
god, whose power seemed to diminish there over the
rest of the year,

to Dionysus because he was precisely what would
allow us, during the darker days, to mitigate this lack
of light, of external heat,

being Bromius, the tumultuous uprising of all our
private ardor, the drunkenness encouraged by drink,
in contrast to the dizziness caused by the immense
brightness beating down on us,

complementary brother of Loxias, showing us the
reverse side of his nature, taking the place of the dazzling, the blind god who is the very blackness of the
light, the inevitable darkness of the revelation,

Dionysus, illumination issuing from the blackness

itself, reason revealed without the help of our delirium, the reddening of the hearth in mid-winter.

8. CASTALIA

Some other time, no doubt after another pilgrimage, I will talk about other gods and other monuments, particular developments of the structure whose center is all I have been able to sketch here.

Then I will broach Poseidon, Athena Pronaia, the nymphs or maenads of the Corcyrian cave, and two of Apollo's enemies, Heracles and Neoptolemus, but I can't end these remarks without at least alluding to the spring of Castalia, because what motivated me to make the journey in the first place, the obscure necessity I was obeying and which preoccupied me for several days precisely because I could not grasp it exactly, finally became clear to me when I reached its famous pure waters:

here, with great pleasure and in long draughts, I drank in the boldness to confront the professorial specter laughing derisively by my side and saying: "What are you doing here? You have almost no Greek left and you never knew much," I drank in the certainty I hadn't had earlier, of the absolute right given me by the response it awakens in me, to apply my own reverent divination to the riddle presented by the immense mouth of rocky gold.

A GLIMPSE OF . . .

MALLIA

I was in Crete, and the day was December 31. I had taken the bus early in the morning in Heraklion to come to this village, a village all of white cubes which lay on the north coast between a mountain covered half way up its slope with olive trees, and orchards that went down to the sea.

I had spent a long time photographing the ruins of an ancient Minoan palace, the circular bases of columns surrounding the courtyard, the several steps, the ball of stone in the middle, all of which was scattered with small white and violet flowers. I had had lunch in a cafe on the side of the road, and I had returned to the bus stop to wait for the bus, well before the hour when it was supposed to come by.

All of a sudden I saw it throbbing towards me

through the dust without slowing down, its roof heavily loaded with bags and baskets. Using the few words of modern Greek that I knew and that I've since forgotten, and throwing in various scraps of other languages that the people I was talking to might have heard, I asked what was happening, if there would be another bus later in the afternoon to take me back to the island's capital. I was told that since this bus was no doubt already completely full, it couldn't take on any new passengers, and that no doubt a second bus would be following along after it. I sat down again. An hour went by.

Then someone explained to me there was no more hope of a bus that day, it was New Year's Eve, and the bus service would be disorganized until the next day.

I couldn't possibly walk back to the city—it was thirty-five kilometers away. The light was going from the sky. The white houses were turning blue.

Some young men went off to one of the largest houses in the village to look for its owner, a rather plump man, by now rather old, who had been to Europe, as they say in Greece, and who apparently spoke English. We had a great deal of trouble understanding each other: what I wanted to find out was where I was going to sleep. It was at this point that everything began to be quite wonderful.

The man in whose cafe I had eaten my bread, mutton and olives that day at about one o'clock had an enterprising son who was dividing the second floor of his house into rooms to be rented during the coming spring and summer; the first room was clean and ready.

I went off down a path with him, and he did the honors of his orchard for me, having me taste all the different kinds of oranges he raised, while the wheel of the windmill above our heads hummed softly, pumping up clear water.

At nightfall, we went down into his basement dining room, where he had me eat dinner with him and his wife and his two daughters, who were about six and seven years old (I was facing the entrance, I saw the steps covered with moonlight, and I have a confused memory of a large pitcher or a face in the stones—I can't remember any more—watching me like some huge, unmoving owl). Then, since it was New Year's Eve, the last night of the year, we played a game with a small six-sided top, betting dried beans, and hardly speaking, naturally, except to pronounce the few simple words, quickly learned, that were needed for the game. We played for several hours, and it was only when the children began to have trouble keeping their eyes open, in spite of their excitement at the presence of a stranger, at the unusual events of the evening, that he took an oil lamp and led me up a creaking outside stairway to the new and very cold room whose windows I could not close.

At dawn I opened the shutters. Below me the leaves of the orange trees trembled in the breeze; the grey sea soughed in the distance.

In the church there was a beautiful iconostasis of

gilded wood; I had no film left for photographing the village; at the end of the morning the bus for Heraklion arrived, at the appointed hour, and I got on, keeping safe in my memory, like a talisman, Mallia's hospitality.

MANTUA

For months I had said to myself: this summer I will
go to Rome for my vacation, to check certain details
there, to steep myself in it more; I can't go anywhere
else for my vacation; but all summer I worked on *La
Modification* without leaving Paris, and when it was finished, when the proofs were corrected, and because I
was tired after this long effort and needed a change of
scene, needed to soak up some sun, I actually did take
a vacation, and I actually did go to Italy, but not to
Rome, because this trip could not have changed anything, and because for the past year and a half, one part
of me at least had been in the train the whole time,
going in that direction, travelling toward that destina-
tion; and so I took the train to Milan, where it rained so
hard all day that after visiting the new museum in

Sforza Castle with the amazing room which was painted with a canopy of interwoven trees under Leonardo's direction, and without even having been able to get into the Sant' Eustorgio Chapel decorated by Foppa which one of my friends has talked to me about so often and for which he feels such undoubtedly justified tenderness, and which I miss every time I go through, I left that very evening for Florence, where for three days I didn't really do anything but sleep, going out only to eat and to shut myself up in a movie theater in the late afternoon, thus seeing, in succession, *I sogni nel cassetone*, the detestable remake of the already detestable *Elle et lui*, and *Les Nuits de Cabiria*.

On the fourth day, I felt rested and it was wonderful October weather, the sun's golden, horizontal rays picking out the hills which I was contemplating from the fortress of the belvedere above the Pitti Palace, this fortress having been restored, cleaned up, completely renovated for an exciting exhibition of detached frescoes; but the very next day I had to go back up north, because I was absolutely determined to see Mantua, stopping off in Modena, a town whose ancient heart spreads out in little winding streets bordered by arcades around one of the most singular and wonderful of all Roman monuments,

Mantua not only because of the *Camera degli Sposi*, but also in order to try to penetrate the secret of the name, which I had encountered so often in books or conversations, and which was marked by an obscure magic that I wanted to understand.

There you are—I would have liked to talk to you about Mantua, about the splendor and desolation of this city a little off from the main roads, without modern buildings or stores, but I don't have either the time or the tranquillity necessary, this evening, to be able to produce anything but the most rudimentary indications, in other words, that it is one of the places, outside of Rome, where the preoccupation with Rome is most obvious, the sort of despair that seized Europe when it began to feel, because of the taking of Constantinople and the discovery of America, that the image of the Empire as world unity was beginning to shatter definitively, desperately trying to camouflage this absence with a furious imitating of "Antiquity," no longer as the foundation of Christianity, the preparation for it, but for the first time as a completely other world from which one was horribly separated and which had to be reconquered (in this respect Mantegna played an exemplary role, as we know).

How struck one is the first time one emerges, after the long preparation of the narrowing Corso, into that dark red group of connecting squares, punctuated by high towers, one of the most remarkably varied of the internal organizations of urban spaces left us by the Middle Ages; how struck by the triumphal arch to the right, of dazzling white marble, which Alberti provided as a porch to his basilica; almost more significant and even more impressive is the other one, sinister, unfinished, of powdery brick, on the square that so correctly bears his name. But only within this labyrinth, at once gloomy and magnificent, so sumptuous, so dilapidated, only when we come to the festive and absurd, disorderly pile of rooms, courts, and gardens which is the Gonzagas' palace at the tip of the city, among the swamps, with its complement on the other side, the Te Palace, does the preoccupation turn into madness and obsession, all the architecure becoming stage sets, with false marbles, false stone, trompe-l'oeil, never enough, never satisfying, the superabundance only accentuating the deception, stage sets in which the life of an entire family, of an entire court, is gradually transformed into theater, "scenes after the manner of the ancients."

And I would have liked to show how the peculiar weight of the Roman theme on Mantua at the time of the Renaissance can be connected to the "spirit of the place" that, for this city, has consistently remained Virgil, represented by a very moving medieval statue in the center:

> e li parenti miei furon Lombardi,
> Mantovani per patria ambedui.
>
> Nacqui sub Julio, ancor che fosse tardi,
> e vissi a Roma sotto il buon Augusto,
> al tempo degli Dei falsi e bugiardi.
>
> Poeta fui, e cantai di quel giusto
> figliuol d'Anchise che venne da Troia
> poi che il superbo Ilion fu combusto.
> (Inferno, I.)

primary poet of Latinity, not only because throughout the Middle Ages he was considered to be the "pagan prophet," the figure representing par excellence what, in Imperial Rome, permitted Christian Rome to exist, but also because his principal work concerned the very origin of Rome, was an attempt, at a time when the latter was realizing that it had become the center of the world, in the place of so many other older cities, to give a mythological justification to this amazing privilege.

At last, leaving Mantua, I rejoined the Orient Express at Verona, another city with handsome interconnecting squares.

FERRARA

Giving up the idea, for the moment, for today, of writing this text on Ferrara as I would have liked to write it, because in order to be specific and illustrate what I want to say I would have to consult documents which are not immediately available to me, for example Roberto Longhi's book *Officina Ferrarese*, which would have provided me with valuable information about the whole group of painters who fascinate me, would have provided photographs, at least, of some of their pictures, which are so rare and so dispersed, of a quality often higher than that of the details of the marvellous Room of the Months at the Schifanoia Palace, allowing us, therefore, to reconstruct much more correctly and more convincingly—taking as a point of departure the architecture as a whole that it suggests to us—this ancient mental world which is so close to us, so rich for us, so precious in its urgent enigma,

documents on the Este family, the nucleus of this whole movement, the nucleus of what can well be called the civilization of Ferrara, documents on all these figures, so singular, and their relations with the masters of the other Italian cities,

on the extinction of this family, on the passing of this city into the hands of the papacy, which signified its final death as place of originality and culture, but which was also no more than the retribution for a long agony that began early in the 16th century, the contamination by the power of Rome, by Rome's seductive artifices, of that spirit which was so profoundly free, so distant from all counter-reformation,

I am resolved to give you only the broad outline of an invitation to discover this place, only my way of using Ferrara, to present you only with fragments of a future text which, if it ever exists, will be somewhat different, as you well know, from what this sketch promises.

We ought to start with the reverberation of the name Ferrara, with the resonance it has had for several centuries in the minds of men who are generally so obscure to us despite their celebrity in schools, who are intelligible only with such difficulty (and this by our own fault, because we knowingly neglect a whole part of their environment), men to whom we apply the quite deceptive name of "classical"; we ought to take Goethe's Torquato Tasso as our starting point and go on to show the prominent role played by the two great writers of Ferrara—Tasso, and before him Ariosto—in the literary equilibrium of Europe, which is to say, in the mental structure of all cultivated Europeans, and, in Italy, of the people too, from the 16th century up to the 19th, and show that the revolt of someone like Boileau against them in France was an incomparably more serious business than a simple question of taste:

> *The terrible mysteries of the faith of Christians*
> *Are not susceptible to gay ornaments.*

There is, in fact, in their poetic practice, a suspension of belief in Christian dogma, which is treated as mythology. In Ariosto, the awareness of this suspension leads to an astonishing irreverence, in the midst of the magical world he describes to us, something that obviously would need to be shown with citations.

This amazing country that one finds in *Orlando Furioso* is the very same one displayed on the walls of the Schifanoia, so much more present. We should, therefore, now turn towards its great quattrocento masters: Tura, Cossa, and Roberti. Clearly, a long commentary on the Room of the Months and its philosophical paganism ought to be inserted here.

There is something in the civilization and spirit of Ferrara that was not followed, a direction that took a sharp turn, stopped abruptly, and found itself in wonderful harmony with certain of our needs, as though all we had to do was to take up this light, which was so bright and which over several centuries gradually darkened, before becoming manifest to us again—as though all we had to do was to take up this light again in order to go forward.

And I will end with what is perhaps most moving about this city, something that will only be discovered by an attentive and patient reading of it: the fact that the group of ancient monuments that draw us to it, for the most part unfinished, and almost all signed by Biagio Rosetti, are really the ruins of a city, but the ruins of a future city which never took place, Ferrara's prosperity abandoning it under pressure from the other states, its boldness becoming blunted, then, as the spirit of all Europe took a different turn, in a direction different from its own, all those neighborhoods planned at the time of its expansion remaining empty, those palaces, designed to form the corners of lively squares, remaining isolated in the middle of wastelands, incomplete stage sets for absent pageants.

Here, then, are real pieces of a dreamed-of city, and among these admirable indications, the traveller's mind may wander as freely and fruitfully as it may wander before the surprising perspectives of the so completely deteriorated paintings of the Schifanoia Palace.

EGYPT

My back is against the wall; it is high time I finally
set to work on the piece about Egypt that I have promised, that I have promised to everything in me that has
become Egyptian to some degree because of the eight
months I spent in the Valley and which reminded me
of this promise so fiercely, and with such shame and
distress during the lamentable events of the past year,
with respect to which certain people—I was abroad—
thought it proper to congratulate me, unaware of the
bonds I want to write about now, and to congratulate
my country for holding up its head at last, as they put
it, that head which was suddenly so . . . and here I need
an adjective to describe disappointment, but one much
stronger than "disappointing," a word to express a real
and completely unexpected betrayal . . . to those who

had placed such an eager, naive confidence in it, a confidence so faithful until then, despite the many obvious bad omens,

for I can say (I will use the word because there isn't any other word for it, even though it has deviated so far from its root and is by now so associated here with so many horrible and insinuating duperies, and I use it very gingerly indeed), that for me Egypt was like a second fatherland, and it was almost a second birth that took place for me there in that elongated belly sucking through its deltaic mouth the Mediterranean and its passing civilizations, hoarding them and amalgamating them in its slow fermentation;

and it is high time, not only because of external urgency, since it is obviously a good idea, in this disastrous haste forced upon us by the scope and rapidity of changes whose reasons and actual dimensions we fail to see most of the time, in this rush to judge which prevents us from thoughtfully examining the facts involved in the problems we would so much like to solve,

to try to bring a little light, a little information, however partial, however weak, however individual it may be, into the area where these dissensions and these questions sprout and take root,

but also because this Egyptian core in myself, if it is still just as active, acts more and more secretly, because it is sinking, more and more deeply covered over by what has happened for me since then,

and because if I don't want to lose track of what I

think and what I see and what I want to say, while these images of Egypt are still sufficiently within my grasp, while I am still able to describe them more or less as I would like to, though already with less precision, I must make a preliminary list of them, a memorandum, a recension.

Now if there is one thing I am quite certain of—and I have known it ever since I returned; for this I didn't even need the conversations I have had since with other people who spent time in Egypt, tourists or businessmen, some of whom were there much longer than I; on rare occasions in Cairo, I had certainly seen some of these compatriots living in Heliopolis or Garden City, profoundly absent from Egypt, blind to Egypt, experiencing its magic only through the most anaesthetizing and deleterious side of it, all the more dangerous, naturally, because one refuses to recognize that it exists—

it is that, if I saw what I saw there, if I had to fight so hard against the power of the deep-seated strangeness of Egypt, if, therefore, I was at that time filled with such a vigorous and lasting passion for it, if I explored, during such an unfortunately limited time and with such curiosity, the old quarters of Cairo, it was because I came from farther away in Egypt, because I didn't live in one of the two large cities in which a European, a young Parisian with a degree in philosophy, would normally live,

and, consequently, I can only begin to talk about Egypt, I can only make myself understood, especially by those who have also lived in Egypt but in completely different conditions, by starting with what my life was like in Minya, then a small city of 80,000 inhabitants in Middle Egypt, two hundred kilometers south of Cairo, on the western bank of the Nile, one of the big cotton markets, without any notable monuments, without any building more than a century old, although the town itself is at least five thousand years old, very likely standing on the same spot as the ancient Monat-Khufu, "nurse" of Cheops, who built the great pyramid,

and although, in any case, whatever the exact identification one might finally manage to give it, some town has always been there, ever since that time, wandering very slowly through the region as its mud brick houses have collapsed, worn away by the wind or eaten away by the very infrequent rains, and as new houses have been built,

down until the one I knew, to the north of which they were hastily constructing tall concrete buildings.

I should say that at that time (King Farouk was still in power; it was his last year; one felt clearly that things could not go on much longer the way they were, but no one dared hope that the blow-up would come so fast) the Egyptian government had decided to make the teaching of French compulsory in the secondary schools just as English was, and, finding themselves faced with a need for more French teachers, and also wanting to do things right (the minister was the blind writer Taha Hussein, the preface for one of whose

books was written by André Gide), through the intermediary of official agencies they had requested that a
contingent of degree-holders, no matter what degrees
they held, be sent to meet this sudden demand.

Wanting to get away, at that time, wanting to with-
draw, and also looking for a bit of adventure, and with
a feeling for Egypt if only because of the Empire-style
fountain across the street from me in the rue de Sèvres,
called the Fountain of the Fellah, I happily allowed
myself to be roped in by that invitation,

endeavoring to be on my guard against the aura of
illusions surrounding the word Orient, telling myself
that everything the romantics went there to find had to
be dead forever, firmly determined not to let myself be
seduced by a certain picturesqueness linked to poverty
and maintained for touristic ends, the Orient of hair-
dressers and boxes of dates; expecting, consequently,
to find nothing in the town where I would be living but
a particularly remote provincial place, particularly
backward in certain respects, but thoroughly banal,
except for the existence of poverties more pronounced,
more visible than anywhere in France, more glaring
wealth perhaps allowing culture and bold thinking for
a few, with a climate warmer than that of Marseilles,
but, since all this required no real effort on my part,
offering me no discoveries (and this entire preliminary
vision would have been completely confirmed if I had
ended up in Alexandria),

bringing with me a trunkful of books that justified
and called for rereading, and my little typewriter be-

cause I intended to write a book which I wasn't able to write there, which I could only write in England, looking back longingly to Egypt.

And so, having arrived at Cairo after an arduous voyage, having taken a room in the Luna Park Hotel, which looked out on a triangular square with a great noisy jet of water in its center, I went to the address I had been given in Paris, to the Ministry of National Education where we were supposed to be received by the man in charge of the teaching of French, an affable and ignorant old Frenchman, satisfied with his lot, established there for years, and who said to me:

"you're supposed to go to Minya; you're lucky; it's a large town with new buildings, big cotton warehouses, a very nice-looking sports club with lovely croquet lawns; it isn't too far from Cairo; you'll see, your life will be very pleasant there; everyone I've sent there has always been very happy."

I also went to see the people to whom I had been given letters of introduction, asking them what they knew of Minya, if they knew anyone there, and they in turn gave me further letters of introduction.

Now, picture the long station platform, with signs bearing the name of Minya spelled out in European letters and also, with superbly thick and supple strokes, in Arabic characters, which I hadn't yet succeeded in identifying and which I've forgotten since,

and the building in the middle similar to the ones you see in the small towns of Languedoc, a stairway going down, a little square, and a perfectly straight street leading to the Nile and bordered by two- and three-story houses painted in wan, washed-out colors.

Only drabness and innocuousness in all this, at first; the weather was nice, it had been nice ever since I had got off the boat, but I didn't see anything surprising in that yet, I was simply enjoying it; it was only little by little that the landscape in which I found myself, and the town that was part of it, and the men living there, under the very thin layer of Europeanization they assumed so carefully, revealed to me their strangeness, slowly, but more and more strongly, so that instead of getting used to it, I lived through my whole stay there with an increasing feeling of being out of place which soon changed into amazement overlaying a feeling of boredom and homesickness, as I appreciated more and more how right the passage from the second book of Herodotus still was that I had translated a few years earlier at the Sorbonne, trying to pass my examination in Greek:

"the Egyptians, who live in a singular climate, on the banks of a river presenting a character different from that of other rivers, have also adopted in almost all things habits and customs opposite from those of other men."

First of all, it's that the space in the Nile Valley has one main direction, an absolutely special direction, something that the composition in ancient Egyptian painting with its superimposed parallels admirably shows us.

If I am in France, I can go away from the place I live,

heading toward any point on the compass; the countryside unfolds all around and even the mountains, certain parts of which are so hard to get to, only seem to us like obstacles, like islands of resistance beyond which everything is all right again; but in Upper Egypt, which is a groove in the Saharan plateau, nine hundred fifty kilometers long if you measure it only from the First Cataract to Cairo, and on the average ten kilometers wide, as long as you go parallel to the course of the Nile, you can travel indefinitely toward Lower Egypt and the Mediterranean in one direction, and in the other toward Ethiopia or the Sudan, but if you set out at right angles to the course of the Nile, you are very soon stopped by the desert, which begins extremely abruptly, without any of the transitions you find in North Africa, and you always know that you will be stopped, because the desert begins with a cliff you can see from wherever you are.

At Minya the Nile flows south to north, and between Cairo, two hundred fifty kilometers to the north, and Assiut, one hundred fifty kilometers to the south, there is no bridge to cross it, and the road that runs along close beside it, forming a boulevard planted with coral trees in full bloom when I arrived in October, which I took every day to go to the Egyptian lycée, learning how full of variety the fine morning weather can be, is the only road that cars other than jeeps can normally travel (there isn't any at all on the other bank), and the narrow town broadens out towards the north, modern buildings being added one next to the other along parallel streets while in the south the mud brick houses

are falling to pieces (Minya must have changed a good
deal since the day I left it; it must have been considera-
bly developed and stabilized, and I would like very
much to go see what sort of face it has now; I knew it as
it was solidifying a little, but it was still in motion, precarious in its poorer neighborhoods, melting away between one's fingers as the villages surely still do and
will do for years, like all things in the Valley, persisting
in its continual demolition, renewing itself for thousands of years now in the dust accumulating from its
ruins), the city squeezed in by the parallel railroad, the
Valley's one line,

and beyond this, among the fields that are like
aquariums filled with liquid wheat because the stalks
are so close together, or planted with cotton, with their
irrigation ditches fed by the shadoof or the Persian
wheel, whose squeaking you can hear accompanied
sometimes, at night, by the rending song of the man
who works them, with those earthen walls delimiting
them, paths on which the men follow each other in a
line, solemnly, one by one, in their white striped or
blue cotton robes, as in the ancient bas-reliefs, so that
of all the paintings the one they most remind one of is
a wonderful part of the third tomb in Beni Hasan, the
burial place of a prominent figure, one of whose titles
was Prince of Monat Khufu, which is famous under the
name of "Caravan of Asians" and often reproduced on
the basis of the diagram Champollion made of it, but
which has never yet to my knowledge been photo-
graphed,

in their robes of white cotton which have turned

gray or brown like their felt skull-caps, like the earth, like the water of the Nile, or like their skin, or like their eyes, the women wrapped in the long black shroud that leaves their feet bare, and that they raise slightly when they enter the water to fill the pale, porous jugs they carry full and cold on their heads, their black shrouds, a fold of which they draw over their laughing faces now and then, with the incomparable bearing they retain even into their old age, the little children often with suppurating eyes, always covered with flies which their mothers stop them from brushing away, their hair shaved off except for a lock or two,

the sheep one by one, the donkeys, the black cow-buffaloes with twisted horns and sometimes the camels sniffing the air, a fox tail hanging at their necks,

and a little farther off, and on the other side of the other fields on the other bank of the broad, slow Nile marked here and there with large triangular sails bellying with the passage of a cooling breeze from the north, or the burning wind of the khamsin in the spring raising swirls of dust and carrying along with it dry insects, scorpions, even small snakes,

the parallel cliffs extend, forming the wall, the proud, irrecusable limit of this damp vegetable word, the abrupt, pitiless frontier of the kingdom of men, the cliffs always visible from everywhere, even during the clear nights, their shadows and their hues varying deliciously every morning according to the angle of the sun and the degree of transparency of the air more or less filled with shining crystalline dust or vapor rising from the river in flood, to the point where I would have liked to keep a journal of these differences,

the endless cliffs interrupted only by extremely rare openings where very uncertain trails lead off, very little frequented trails, phantom trails towards extremely rare oases or distant ports, distant abandoned mines,

edge of the valley up which we climbed, slipping through the dried bed of a wadi, my friends and I, French teachers who had arrived at about the same time I had, in the same conditions, who had come from different places and were versed in different areas of knowledge, like a handful of pebbles thrown into the long crucible, two of whom in particular, one a grammarian, the other an historian, I am so grateful to for having helped me to live "in" Egypt, which involved very hard work, a relentless surveillance of ourselves, keeping our eyes open in spite of the constant temptation to yield to the prevailing somnolence, who so supported me in my passion to see things (I have lost all trace of one of them, who may still be there and who I hope will some day read what I have written here),

we climbed without worrying about the surprise of our Egyptian colleagues or the students who went with us, acting as guides and sometimes putting us up at their parents' farms,

because we wanted to know how it went on afterward, because, having arrived from Europe, we didn't understand that it didn't go on, that something quite different began, a space in which we were nothing, like the surface of another planet, that a few steps away from the most intensive cultivation in the world, from those fields producing three harvests a year, all at once, without the slightest transition, we encountered nothing but rock worn by the wind, the dry crust of the globe,

fairly often at first, then less and less often, as the lesson was gradually learned,

gazing always with the same almost scandalized disappointment at the immense sterile spaces without grass, without trees, without roads or towns, knowing that they continued without any perceptible interruption (a few infinitesimal green islands, in hollows, in the middle of this petrified ocean that was not navigable, where one couldn't swim, where one couldn't breathe) on one side as far as the Red Sea, on the other as far as the Atlantic,

so that, of course, any desire we might have had in our ignorance, then in our forgetfulness, while we were still down below, to enter it, to plunge into it, to take walks there, enjoying the landscape, to find relaxation there in its hoped-for variety, faded away,

because we would have needed some distinctive point, a grotto, peak or ruin, something allowing us to organize the space around it, fit it into our human plans, providing us with reasons for choosing one or another of the innumerable directions that all looked equivalent to us, attaching it to the valley, whereas, as we knew, there was nothing out there, nothing for us, nothing accessible, that whether we took one step, ten steps, a hundred, to the right or the left, it was all the same,

and so that our walking, starting from this very visible boundary line, could no longer have either any meaning or any purpose (what was the use of making our way painfully over this bare, hilly plateau, or, in other spots, through this sand, under the sun, without hope of shadow or spring, for one kilometer or five, without even reaching that first fold in the ground, to find nothing more than the monotony of this uninhabited stone that we could already see spread out before us, and then come back?),

realizing that it was the domain of the gods and the dead, an immense elsewhere close by, without names, without landmarks, and without maps, an immense reserve of menace which could sometimes take on a form and invade the dreams of Egyptians in the shape of devastating phantoms, or jackals appearing at nightfall with shining eyes, or wild animals breaking into stables and sheep-folds, and pillagers (here the nomads can only survive by brigandage; parasites on the valley, they are, for those who inhabit it, living people who even before death already have a spectral, ghostly existence) or a parching wind,

a sacred domain both because of its dazzling permanence on the horizon of daily occupations, above the fields, at the ends of streets, and because of its so distinctly separate nature,

after which we could only turn our eyes back to the valley at our feet, its mosaic of cultivated plots, of squares of different shades of green which became more and more luminous, like a large habitable stained glass window, as evening approached, toward this landscape with its horizontal registers, to the great Nile reflecting the sky and the sun from here, to the road and the train, to the town and its crowd, in front of the other cliff and the pure sky.

This fundamental direction of space is all the more powerfully felt because in Minya, and in almost the entire valley except for the segment from Qenan to Girga, where the Nile runs more or less from east to west (but even there, the mentality of the neighboring regions is so contagious that this appears to be an anomaly, like a singular fold in the compass card, a momentary torsion of the whole space), every day one can follow the course of the sun as it moves perpendicular to this terrestrial axis and hardly varying in a sky that is almost always very clear, without anything to cloud it, born every morning after a thin fringe at the summit of the eastern cliff catches fire, appearing and brightening above a point that is always predictable, with the same rapidity, the same sureness of flight as the black scarab beetles used by the ancient hieroglyphics to designate it in its youth, in its first hours, and which children unearth in their play, striking the east side of objects in houses and the trunks of trees, and then, every evening, he who had been so dazzling, so lofty, so motionless above the river at midday, Horus with wings outspread petrifying men's motions with his terrible eye, causing the wings of the kites above us to become transparent, or Aton caressing them with his numberless hands at the tips of his rays as he is portrayed in the Amarnian monuments, would reach the west, sink and darken more and more quickly, fall truly as though snapped up by an immense mouth, then melt in a horizon of bloody dust that turns violet before abruptly giving way to the night, the temperature immediately falling so that in winter, with a feeling of abandon, you are suddenly seized by the cold—and you have to button up your coat even though you wouldn't even have thought of putting it on just a short time before—and in springtime life can start happily,

as the calm moon takes over, a power among the voluminous stars, incomparably more numerous and closer than in our country, standing out against the black sky, and appearing, according to its phase, either round, celebrated by all the wrinkles of the Nile, or with its two points in the air like a pair of horns, like a boat, down below like the arch of a bridge, like a door, like the beak of an ibis,

on which the Moslems base their calendar, while Europeans and Copts base theirs on the sun a little differently, so that each day has several dates, the feast days of the various faiths drawing closer together or moving farther apart, the years and the months rolling along gently one across the other like the oiled gears of an immense, silent machine,

in the sky, which is almost always clear since in this region, they say, it rains, on the average, two hours a year (in Luxor the joke is that the last downpour they had there was the announcement of the Napoleonic expedition), and since, although we had already seen clouds, already seen drops of water fall for a few minutes and then evaporate even as they approached the hot ground and the dry dust, just once (I remember, I was at the home of one of my French friends), an extraordinary noise tore us from our reading, a sound like a drumroll, which at first we couldn't figure out, then seeing, flabbergasted, that this transformation in the air, these shouts in the street, this was rain, real rain, with an unheard of violence and illuminated by the sun; just once we had been able to watch it working away for almost an hour, as drunk as though each of those drops of water were a drop of alcohol, after which, the clouds having dispersed, the streams having dried on the ground, where they had carved complex furrows, we learned that several houses had been damaged in the southern quarter,

this fundamental organization so evident that to show to you where a particular place is, an apartment in a building, for example, they don't use your position at the moment as a reference point, but those constants of the landscape identical to the cardinal points, those absolute landmarks which even the walls of a room can't hide; and that, consequently, they will not say to you, Take your first left, then turn right, but, Take the first street to the east, then turn north, go up the stairs, and it's the south door; that at the table one will even speak of a chair that is to the west of another chair.

In opposition to the sacred domain of the sky and the desert, this domain of divine permanence and its clear movements on which everything must be regulated, Upper Egypt itself, the back of the Valley where the people live, "the black earth," which hasn't in the least always been there, but is a gift of the Nile, this very soil on which one lives, which one cultivates, from which one draws one's sustenance, being already a "production" whose slow accumulation one can note each year, this soil so precious that sometimes, in order not to waste a single acre, the villages form little enclaves in the desert, minuscule excrescences, is entirely governed by precariousness, by a continual deterioration against which one must constantly fight if one wants to maintain anything whatever already achieved.

Everything here seems ephemeral, men certainly, and all the domestic animals, but also the very configuration of the terrain, of these fields that used to be covered every year by the dark and nourishing waters (only the towns emerging, says Herodotus, with almost the same effect as the islands in the Aegean Sea), of these fields whose borders had to be redrawn by a whole army of surveyors every time the river fell, borders which were engulfed and obliterated, now, certainly, for the most part remaining at all seasons beyond reach of the overflowing river, already regularized by the first dams, but in the middle of which, nevertheless, I saw, as it subsided, banks of sand and earth form, without one being able to predict where, soon true islands, dry in a few days, their black surfaces fissuring into deep crevices in all directions like an intense, amorous penetration by the air and the sun, then worked by the fellahs leaning on their wooden plows behind their asses or female buffaloes, then sprout, turn green, grow their quick, dense crops, islands that one never thought of giving any particular name to, since one knew that at the next return of the waters they would be unrecognizable again.

Faced with such a manifest division of the universe, this landscape of contrasts, how natural it was that the ancient Egyptians should have considered that if it was to be stable, the organization of their society also had to integrate a contrast, had to be based on a balance of opposed parts, and that they should have hailed as "their first king who was a man," as the first successor to the gods, Min or Menes who succeeded in bringing together on his head the crowns of two regions as visibly distinct as Upper and Lower Egypt, linking this event to the construction of a dike to protect from the flood a site on which to build a permanent capital in the middle of the "earth";

faced with this constant humiliation of the near world by another world, how natural it was that they should have believed that the pharaoh, that maintainer, came from the family of the gods, and that under his direction they should have spent such a fabulous sum of work to allow him to assure them of where he came from and who he belonged to by leaving a mark of his reign, of his presence, a mark as obviously lasting as possible, a monument of human fabrication but capable of rivaling in mass the desert escarpments, in conformance with the laws of this divine world, the pyramid oriented according to its fundamental direction, four-sided, its polished faces corresponding exactly to the cardinal points, whose top was lit in the morning not only before anything else in the valley, but even before the edge of the cliff, dazzling at midday, reflecting horizontally the almost vertical rays, the true earthly image of the sun, looming in the evening in front of us as it sinks in the sky, like a mask before its face as it dies, like the door to its tomb;

how natural it is, consequently, that among all the lands of the ancient Orient, it should be in Upper Egypt that the most numerous, the most impressive, and above all the best preservd ruins stand.

*

The day after I arrived in Minya, I went to see a cotton buyer whose address I had been given, an aging Jew from Alexandria who advised me, since I wanted to settle somewhere, to rent part of an apartment.

Actually, one of his accountants, who spoke very good French, had just found one that he would be happy to share with me.

This was how I met Hassan, who acted as a sort of steward to me throughout my stay and who now took me into an empty, tiled, high-ceilinged room with cement walls painted green which soon became punctuated with little spots of blood up to a certain height, because it was autumn, the waters of the Nile were just beginning to go down, and as a result there were swarms of very irritating mosquitoes which I would squash before I went to sleep.

We hired a man with a cart to move my trunk, then we went off to look for a bed, which wasn't hard to find because the year before, I believe, the hospital had ordered a few more than it had room for,

a metal bed with a noisy bedspring of wires.

At a cloth merchant's we chose some material for the mattress, thick and silky with gray stripes, like the material from which the farmers made their robes; we got samples of raw cotton at the warehouse and we entrusted the lot to someone who did sewing.

Then we bought a pair of sheets and a bedspread, so that the next day I was able to move into the apartment whose only other piece of furniture was Hassan's big double bed and, on the floor of the alcove that served as a kitchen, a Primus stove,

(a pitcher, a water-bottle, a few pink-flowered china plates, a few glasses and some silverware, two pots with lids).

Nor did I have any trouble finding chairs, because the "sports club" had ordered quantities of them for its garden; but I needed still other objects in that room; I felt it was impossible to live without a table, needing one to read and write, do my job, however elementary, as teacher, needing it even for eating comfortably.

Now if the richest Egyptians of Minya had quantities

of heavy, stupidly sumptuous pieces of furniture in their homes—thickly gilded, in an overloaded Louis XV style, covered in boldly-flowered cretonne—they generally ordered it from Cairo, or even directly from the big stores in Paris and London, and at that time there wasn't one table to be bought in the whole city.

Because of the delays of the royal government, I had very little money at the beginning of my stay, and so the only solution was to have a table made by one of those actually quite skillful carpenters who took so much pride in their painstakingly produced fretwork for sideboards they hoped would be able to measure up to the ones occasionally unloaded from the train,

to buy the wood, to make a working drawing showing exactly how I wanted it,

then to go to the workshop every day for three weeks, learning patience and the fact that it simply wasn't possible to find an Arab equivalent for the words *too late*, to see how the job was coming along,

until the time when at last I saw it, the longed-for table, varnished, with a drawer, as I had specially requested, but standing much too high, so that I had to have its legs sawed down, and then sawed down again, before I could use it.

Then we undertook to have another similar table made for the dining room, whose installation we celebrated with a banquet; then, encouraged by these handsome successes, I went so far as to order and make a precise drawing for a small cupboard that was finished either before or after the Christmas holidays, I don't remember which, the dimensions I had given having been respected but inverted, where I was at last able to put away, safe from the dust, my clothes and my books, which I hadn't really been able to take out of my trunk since I left Paris.

And so these objects, which were so familiar, which I had taken for granted in France, to which my every-day activities were so tied, which I knew I could do without for a while, during the holidays, while camping, but which I was absolutely sure of finding again a few days later, when I returned to normal life, to my work,

which were a fundamental given of the world I belonged to, which existed in all dwellings without exception, whose presence and the need for which were absolutely the rule,

here seemed to me to be the result of a long desiring, a sort of extraordinary luxury, associated with a rich class that had the leisure to order them from Europe or wait interminably for local craftsmen to make imitations of them,

as the result of a whole special cultural evolution.

When I walked through the streets of the villages, I could see the insides of the houses, more or less empty but for the Primus stove, a few jars, a mat and some coverlets;

when I walked through the streets of Minya, which at first seemed so like the sad streets of towns in the South of France, I knew that inside these buildings the furnishings in the rooms were utterly rudimentary compared to the ones I needed, whose existence was implied by my habits and my way of being,

that my Egyptian colleagues, dressed like me, and even, I must say, much more carefully than I, therefore had, when they returned home, a routine behavior that was completely different from mine.

I knew some who lived in apartments like the one I lived in, with several members of their families who were pupils at the lycée, with a single desk for all of them, which they used one at a time, with their freshly washed shirts arranged in a pile on the tile floor in one corner, covered with a piece of paper to protect them a little from the dust, their suits hanging one on top of another from a nail driven into the wall, like Hassan's in the room next to mine.

Considering all that, how could I not marvel at the table?

How could I not see that to speak of this simple object is also to posit an entire civilization of a certain kind, an entire area of history, and that the introduction of such objects into a culture where they are alien, or what amounts to the same thing, the adoption of a European-style education, absolutely inevitable because of the latter's obvious technical superiority, that is, an education that implies among other things the existence of these objects, that calls for them when they aren't yet there, causes a gigantic perturbation and disarray even in the most everyday behavior.

Theoretically, secondary education was compulsory

and free, even the books, indeed all the educational material being provided by the State, and every day a free lunch was served: sandwiches stuffed with halvah, that oily and sandy gray sweet of all Eastern Mediterranean countries, oranges or bananas, at first in the classrooms themselves, which produced an indescribable disorder, then outdoors,

but this compulsoriness remained purely theoretical, and in actuality the education was reserved for a quite small fraction of the population, because, in order to be admitted into the precincts of the lycée, the pupils had to wear a European suit, long pants, shirt, tie, jacket, socks and shoes, which very few farmers could afford.

So it was that I would find myself facing classes of forty to fifty students between the ages of fourteen and twenty whose names I could not only not manage to remember, but in the beginning not even repeat or transcribe,

who had all had some French already, in principle, but most of whom didn't know a single word, I at first not knowing a word of Arabic, not knowing even the alphabet, which I took a long time to learn and afterwards forgot.

They generally knew a little English, and I did too, but we pronounced it in such different ways that it was a very precarious means of communication. We were therefore reduced to the direct method in its most primitive form, one of the only effective methods of explanation being drawing pictures.

Soon half the students, realizing they would never

learn French under such conditions, gave up for good, installing themselves in the back of the room to play cards peacefully or memorize the textbooks they at least had the possibility of reading, while the others came up close to me and began to make some progress,

for which they deserved all the more credit since there reigned a continuous agitation and noise which I could do nothing about, first of all because if I mentioned it to the other teachers they were astonished at my astonishment, considering this state of things to be perfectly normal and unavoidable, the students always answering, sincerely surprised, that they always did this in the other classes, which was true,

and because, on the other hand, there was no system of punishments besides the whip, administered by a policeman who was always walking in the hallway, truncheon at his belt and handy, ready to come to the aid of teachers in distress, a method too contrary to my French habits for me ever to be able to decide to use it, but which was not distasteful to my colleagues, in their moments of ill temper, so that now and then one heard some long resigned howls.

For example, from time to time I would see two students who were very good friends and always sat next to each other stand up, their eyes blazing, though nothing had given any warning of the coming storm, grab each other, roll in the aisle showering each other with blows and tearing each other's clothes while the others looked on, not even very interested, simply accustomed to it,

then, after a few moments, rarely more than a minute, get up feeling calmer, brush off their jackets, sit down next to each other again as though nothing had happened, continue to follow the lessons sharing the same book, because often one of them had forgotten or lost his;

and afterwards I would try to find out about it from the others, who answered me graciously, always amused at my preposterous curiosity, that they belonged to two neighboring villages between whom for a very long time there had been disputes whose origin no one was very sure of any more, or most often, that one was a Moslem, with sometimes a little lion tattooed on the back of his hand, and the other a Copt, with almost always a little cross tattooed on his wrist, that they were certainly very good friends, but that they were clearly obliged, from time to time, to have things out, to settle, temporarily, differences that were not theirs personally but in the midst of which they found themselves caught.

The religious landscape of Minya was very complex:

confronting Islam, which was almost monolithic where doctrine and ritual were concerned, but within which one found a great diversity of attitudes towards the observance of practices, very few people following them strictly, or of the prohibitions, the more or less frequent, more or less public use of wine being very closely connected with membership within this or that social group, all joining in the at least public obedience to the rules of Ramadan,

there were a host of Christian sects and churches in

perpetual disagreement, first of all the orthodox Copts, quite numerous and powerful, proud of how long they had been in the Valley, endeavoring to compete with the Moslems in the austerity of their fasting, but on Easter celebrating their spiritual independence by dazzling bouts of drunkenness, with superb, extremely long and dramatic ceremonies whose canon remained in that Coptic language inherited from the ancient Egyptians, the rest translated into Arabic, accompanied by wonderful hoarse chants led by a Moslem who was always blind, a blind child next to him learning the job little by little, small cymbals and a triangle beating out the rhythm,

then the Roman Catholics with Coptic rituals, the Greek Orthodox, the Greeks having preserved ever since Herodotus an almost complete monopoly on the spice trade in Egypt, the Roman Catholics with Greek rituals, the Maronites, the Roman Catholics with Roman rituals represented at that time by two schools: one, an elementary school for boys, in the south of the city, in full decline, run by Jesuits, French-speaking though for the most part Syrians, and which at least had in its library a complete edition with translations of the works of Saint Augustine; the other, for girls, run by nuns who were also French-speaking but who came from all sorts of countries (there was notably one wonderfully beautiful Mexican), teaching that "our ancestors the Gauls had blue eyes and blond hair" and who also had what was to us a treasure in their library, the *National Geographic Magazine*, maybe about ten Protestants sects, some of English origin, others of American origin, imported at the same time as the agricultural machinery,

and lastly, of course, a scattering of Jews.

But all these "official" religions in discreet conflict, especially the two main ones—Islam and Coptic Christianity—with rare explosions in the midst of general tolerance, were in communication through a whole fabric of beliefs and practices that one could call superstitious, whose diffuse presence one was constantly aware of, but about which it was often difficult to obtain information, our pupils and our colleagues being afraid that we Europeans would react with mockery, they themselves being ashamed of them, no longer adhering to them, of course, in their fully conscious moments, but always obscurely subject to their magic, and not managing to detach themselves sufficiently from them to be able to view them with ethnographic objectivity,

practices and beliefs which, when they came into patent conflict with the two great religions, when they were forbidden and secret, having as a consequence the status of witchcraft, were naturally connected for the believers of one with the presence of the other, so that the most effective magician for the Moslems was as a rule of Coptic persuasion, Moslem for the Christians,

were naturally connected for everyone in every case to the ruins of the ancient monuments, particularly scandalous to the strict Moslems, more and more rare, because of the innumerable figures that decorated them, vestiges for everyone of the world where Joseph had ruled, from which Moses had fled.

Thus, to the plurality of religions present, felt, moreover, to be part of an historic sequence, Coptic Christianity considering itself as coming after the Jewish religion, Islam as coming after the Jewish and Christian revelations, the Protestant sects and even Roman Catholicism appearing here as latecomers closely connected with the European invasion, as the return of a Christianity that had evolved differently elsewhere, all religions including a certain number of shared sacred figures, having in common a certain reference to ancient Egypt,

was therefore added the confusedly but very strongly sensed presence of another, older religion, something dark and dangerous in the background, but haunted by a strange wisdom, and this, not only because it is actually possible to show a continuity between ancient beliefs and practices and a good part of current superstitions, but because this continuity was felt as such owing to the endurance of the monuments, if not at Minya itself, then at least in the region, and owing to the role they played in witchcraft or at least had still played a few years before,

felt as such especially in certain completely public customs, for example the feast of Cham al Nessim, "the smell of the breeze," the biggest feast of the year because it was the only one celebrated by the whole population without distinction (there were a few politi-

cal anniversaries, naturally, but their celebrations were
nothing like this), the theoretical date of the beginning
of the dry, hot wind, calculated according to the Coptic
Moslem calendar, the calendar, I was told by a land-
owner of the environs of Minya whose wife was
French, which he himself had to refer to in his agricultural work, because it was based on that of the ancient
Egyptians, which was developed in this same valley,

a festival that marked the beginning of spring (one
spent all night outdoors, in new clothes, with flowers
and onions over all the doors), that is, which corresponded to a complete transformation of daily life for
which nothing had prepared me, day and night
abruptly changing roles, the afternoon, which soon became torrid, henceforth being devoted to sleep, an ex-
hausted sleep on a mattress which had to be dried in
the evening when I woke up because it was soaked
through with sweat, life beginning at sunset, the
streets, empty until then, suddenly coming alive with a
gaiety that hadn't existed during the winter,

and fragrances taking on an importance, a volume,
that they never have in Europe, the smells of flowers
and fruits, which made you turn your head in the street
as though they were calling out to you, the smells of
animals and men, and most of all the smell of corpses
which penetrated everything, which was in earth and
water, which remained attached to your clothes when
you had passed near a cemetery, whether they were
recent or thousands of years old, pleasant or disagreeable smells, sometimes so heady that I said to myself

that if Saint Augustine had lived in Upper Egypt in the springtime, he wouldn't have been able, when enumerating in the tenth book of the *Confessions* the temptations he was exposed to, and when describing to us the different sorts of concupiscence, to tell us so simply, and with some surprise and distrust of himself, that "the seductiveness of fragrances leaves him rather indifferent."

From that time on, the school also had a changed look, the teaching began to disintegrate when confronted with this violent rejuvenation of all things, the students turning up less and less often, the last of the faithful taking out of their pockets, when they arrived, handfuls of little roses they had picked on the way, so that in the end we didn't go to school any more except to verify that the classrooms were empty;

and if they didn't come any more it wasn't only because they wanted to sleep or take a walk, it was more than anything because they were terrified of the approaching exams, even though the richest of them shouldn't have had anything to worry about, since everything in Egypt at that time, without exception, could be bought, and they prepared feverishly in little groups, learning their textbooks by heart from cover to cover, reciting them sitting in a circle at night in the streets around each streetlight, because many of them had no electricity in their homes, and preparing memory aids for themselves with wonderful care, "aspirins," as they called them, squares of white paper kept in their palms, covered with very tightly packed fine lines of that admirable writing which, reduced to its principal elements, constitutes its own stenography.

To help them in this considerable effort of memorizing—and it must be understood that if they were reduced in this way to learning by rote, it wasn't only through a carry-over from the habit of Koranic teaching, where the sacred text plays a much more important role than the Bible in Christian religions, being not only inspired by God, but his eternal word itself, so that recitation becomes the religious act par excellence,

but it was also because this knowledge that they were asked to acquire and that they wanted so much to acquire because it was obviously the key to power, most of the time formed extremely circumscribed little islands in their minds, which virtually did not communicate with their personal experience,

(to take an extreme example, I remember examining students in a Southern city for the Egyptian baccalaureate, which involved a whole program, in imitation of the French one, of geography, physics, etc., asking them questions about a passage from the French book that seemed to me very simple, which had to do with a railroad train, and realizing that they had never seen one because they came from a college situated in a small town on the other side of the river and had crossed the river for the first time on the occasion of their examination),

in their minds and in the minds of most of their teachers and examiners, so that it would have been useless for the latter to pose additional questions, or to ask for supplementary details, because, as they well knew, since there were always a few who would try it, they would only have been answered by a confession of ignorance naturally accompanied by a fit of ill humor,

islands that pulverized the habits of thinking that surrounded them, just as the machines, the furniture, the clothes imported from Europe, all those emblems of power, pulverized the old habits around them, though this did not mean that the "European-style life" for which these objects had been made could be established throughout the whole country,

gradually shaking all the beliefs, but without being able to obliterate or replace them, leaving them defenseless, in a kind of chaotic mental emptiness with, in certain of my colleagues, a terrible feeling of frustration, which could find no outlet except in the still very distant hope that one day it would be possible to wrest from Europe every last one of its mysteries and that then you would be able to get your revenge and beat it on its own ground,

islands which remained separated from one another, and which in some sense floated, too obviously incomplete, full of lacunae, without managing to organize themselves stably and coherently in relation to what they saw, in relation to the crumbling world they came from, amidst the wreckage of which they lived—

therefore, in order to help them in this considerable effort, in order to fix their attention better on these words and phrases often so barely intelligible, many

111

mixed hashish in cigarettes and smoked it, drugging themselves with it, though its use was officially forbidden, so that the surest way to obtain it without risk was to apply to the policemen, the prohibition thus creating, in practice, a State monopoly,

with hashish, whose extremely widespread use, beyond these scholarly applications, evidently played an important role in the equilibrium of the Egyptian mentality, not only because it was a little less clearly prohibited than the use of alcohol in the prescriptions of the Koran, but more importantly because the cold high it induces, which leaves the lid firmly on a person's dreams, would allow the disoriented consciousness a marvellous rest, masking its own devastation from it by a sort of inward flight, by the happy contemplation, in the moment, of the objects, the landscape, the arrangement of reality which, when one returned, sobered, to one's daily chores, appeared so inexplicably fissured, shaky, here and there so strangely foreign and obscure,

what you contemplate then, in your intoxication, isolating you, filling you, pushing back into the shadow all your relations with the rest.

I certainly can't boast of any great experience with hashish, since I felt a good deal of distrust of it in the beginning, obviously afraid of acquiring a taste for it (it was a subject that occupied an important place in our conversations, and at that time my friends and I carefully consulted the passages in *Les Paradis artificiels* that talk about it), and I only felt the full effects of it one time, one night, in the spring, on the way back from a visit we had paid to the uncle of one of our students, long hours passed in an orchard doing nothing, saying almost nothing, tasting little strangely tart fruits, and watching the branches of the trees or the palms swaying, a veil passing on the other side of the wall.

It was at the home of the parents of another student who lived halfway back from there, more or less a cousin of the first, with whom he had arranged to prepare this little party for us in a tiny courtyard, below street level, illuminated by an oil lamp, surrounded by benches, I think (certain details of this scene have remained present in my mind with a wonderful distinctness, others, though I need them to show how all this was arranged, have completely disappeared into vacancy, they have sunk forever into the vacancy to which they were already relegated that night the moment the intoxication began),

with a few embers glowing in an earthenware plate, with one of the students standing in a gray robe, in profile, resplendent in his pride as host, with the faces of the women appearing furtively in a doorway, smiling, intrigued, startled, drawing their black veils back over their faces, with a policeman, his red tarboosh on his head,

and the amazing stars above, and the stirring of the air, the rustling of the leaves, that kind of breathing of the water and the sleepers, men and animals, which one heard, and that smoke smelling of eucalyptus that we drank greedily from the reed stem of the chibouk, that great pipe with its water filter, which passed from mouth to mouth, and the sweets that one was always offered at these times;

so, yes, I felt it, that exaltation, my eyes dilated, and on my face appeared that fixed smile that is so easy to recognize, and everything I saw overwhelmed me by its beauty;

and of course I understand that when you remember the pleasure you were made to feel by the glorious detachment of these same objects and faces which, when you consider them now in the midst of your problems, your mental distress, no longer succeed in delivering you from them, you may have the impression of a veil interposing itself between them and you, a veil Indian hemp dissipates, and that a legend like that of the Paradise of Assassins could have come into being,

but as far as I'm concerned, I know very well that as soon as these effects began to wear off, what immediately invaded me was a feeling of discontent and frustration, because I should have been able to experience this beauty, this emotion, even without the power of this weed,

(I was in the middle of the Valley at night, we were returning on foot to Minya), but it was impossible for me to judge to what extent exactly,

because that beauty, as a consequence, far from having been given to me as I had had the illusion it was, all of a sudden had been denied me, whereas I could have attained it,

because I was obliged to mark those few hours, de-

spite their radiance, which endures even today, with a
symbol of doubt, just as one marks an uncertain passage in a text with an obelus.

As for the students—the teachers for their part not
having the means to procure themselves these little
brownish green cubes very often—it is clear that from
the moment they became however confusedly aware
of the role their habitual use was beginnning to play,
no longer innocent stimulation of the pleasure of being
in society, but worsening fragmentation of the knowledge they wanted to acquire, aggravation of the mental
disorder they were suffering,

it is clear that they grew ashamed of this sterile
comfort, that the very pleasures it procured for them
turned rotten,

because falsehood and vanity continued to leer out
at them from the shadows around the luminous objects,

and because, as a consequence, their secret resentment of Europe deepened, their envy, their uneasiness,
their painful, silent need for a reshaping of the whole
configuration of the world, naturally taking into account all that Europe contributed, but not something
that boiled down to a mere adoption of that contribu-
tion in the form it came in.

*

This insidious strangeness, this cunning dissolution,
in which I felt myself threatened with asphyxia and
lethargy, in which everything risked turning into a

drug and a pretext for somnolence, a pretext for avoiding all of this so visible unhappiness—in the beginning, I escaped it as often as possible, fleeing from the
school every weekend, fleeing from the school at noon
every Thursday as soon as the bell rang, because for us
Friday took the place of Sunday, just barely catching
the train for Cairo to breathe a little of the cooler air
from the West,

to recover an image of it that was a little less carica-
tured, a little less thin, a little less dislocated than the
image whose ravages I saw in Minya,

in order that the dreadful perturbation caused by
our mere presence, our gestures, our ohs and ahs, our
questions, our explanations, be got into the best possible focus, running off to movie theaters to see films I
probably wouldn't have gone to see in Paris, but which
nevertheless formed an approximation,

haunting bookstores and lending libraries, delight-
ing in the presence of shops, posters, and tramways.

But soon, as I came to feel closer to Egypt, beginning
to see this landscape, at last, in its difference, the faces
that surrounded me in their splendor and their unhappiness,

as the feeling of my involuntary guilt became
sharper and sharper in this night, this perdition which I
caught more and more clearly in those at once confident and envious eyes that observed me and ques-
tioned me, of my original sin, in some sense, as a
European,

as I began to become Egyptian myself, sufficiently

steeped in these dissonances to find that I too was faced with an imperious need to attenuate them, to introduce a little order and clarity in the menacing confusion, to become a little better acquainted with the terrain where there was taking place a devastation in which I myself had a hand ineluctably,

the need, consequently, to situate correctly in relation to one another the dissociated elements whose shreds were all I could see in Minya,

soon it wasn't only a return to Europe that I went to seek in Cairo, but the city's admirable analysis of the different elements present in the life and mentality of Egypt, its wonderful exhibit of the successive civilizations to which these elements were attached.

For although it is of course completely wrong to say, as Nerval does, that Cairo is "the only Eastern city where one can rediscover the clearly distinct layers of many historical ages," this "distinctness" is certainly clearer here than in the others (much clearer today, what is more, than at the time of Nerval's journey), and this, as he was quite aware, because of the durable nature of its monuments, of its princes' obsession with endurance:

"the mosques alone tell the whole story of Moslem Egypt, for each prince had at least one built, wanting to hand down the memory of his time and his glory forever; the names of Amru, Hakim, Tulun, Saladin, Bibars or Barkuk are thus preserved in the people's memory."

The durability of its buildings, which makes Cairo

so unusual among the cities of Moslem Egypt, all doomed, until the arrival of concrete, to see their sun-dried bricks crumble away, is the reason for the way its different quarters are so neatly juxtaposed, so that to cross certain streets is to go from one time to another, from one mental world to another.

Thus, along the magnificent Nile with its islands and their gardens, close to its bifurcation into a delta, there àre the rich, European-style neighborhoods, with their arrow-straight avenues bordered by large, modern, reinforced concrete blocks of offices and apartments, with a fever of construction everywhere which has certainly increased even more since I left Egypt, so that the look of the main squares must have changed con-siderably,

with the movie theaters and their lighted signs, their immense placards painted all colors of the rainbow, the Paris-style store windows, the English-style tea-rooms, the restaurants for tourists, the travel agencies, the grand hotels with their "pharaoh" or "thousand and one nights" decors, always inspired in fact by wretched Western degradations of the works of art of these two worlds, even though they were only a few steps away and so easy to consult, for example Shep-heard's Hotel, since burned down, as I was not dis-pleased to learn, I must confess,

with the tramways, the taxis, nearly all dark blue, almost black Chevrolets at that time, with loudspeak-ers shouting Arab adaptations of American songs,

and certain more tranquil areas, planted with trees,

with gently winding streets, with separate houses, the private residences belonging to the embassies,

from time to time kites wheeling above the cross-roads, and in a passageway, reminding you it was there as though by the sounding of a gong, the dazzling cliff of the moqattam through the dust.

To the north of this area, which its inhabitants, Europeans or rich, Europeanized Egyptians, virtually never left except to go to elegant suburbs of the same type, Heliopolis or Helwan,

on the other side of the station, losing itself little by little in the spreading reaches of Lower Egypt, lay Shubra, Cairo's Aubervilliers, where of course nothing remained of the rose gardens, the alleys, and the pavillion that so delighted Nerval,

an enormous, teeming, black outlying district, with nothing left of the festive din of the elegant and lazy capital one had just left, nothing but the rumbling, harsh and desperate monotony of the poorly industrialized suburbs, with smoke, the smell of gas and detergents, the puddles, the broken windows, the famished cats with elongated muzzles, as in the ancient statues, whom no one dares to destroy.

Then, parallel to the Nile, to the cliff, and to this whole first recent city, to this city you come upon first, already so divided, some parts so brilliant and others so miserable,

pierced by a few straight avenues to ease the traffic, otherwise all little streets where cars can't go through, beginning almost as abruptly as the desert with something menacing about it, still surrounded by part of its old ramparts with three magnificent gates,

reigns medieval Cairo, the one Lane and Nerval saw in its already dilapidated splendor, the one into which even the Cairo tourists didn't dare to venture except rarely and in groups because among the inhabitants of those neighborhoods there was a terrible mistrust of the desecrating, frivolous stranger,

so that if, by the end of my stay, we were able to feel altogether at ease strolling there, going into mosques without buying tickets, staying there as long as we liked, it was because for us they had become true objects of pilgrimage, because our few months in Minya had already led to our assimilation into the landscape, our way of walking and looking at things was in harmony with that of other people, so that for these caretakers, these tradesmen, these people who passed us in the street, although we certainly didn't have the appearance of Egyptians, we also no longer corresponded in the least to the type of European they hated, so that they would ask us, amused at our ignorance of Arabic, whether we were Turks or Persians.

For the resentment against Europe was concentrated in the shadow and under the protection of those innumerable mosques, almost all of which, unfortunately, were cracked, halfway abandoned, needing an enormous amount of repair work, with their architecture that was so noble and so strict, their superb severity sometimes enriched at certain points by the most whimsical evolutions, with the exalting geometry of their Kufic inscriptions, all of this so admirably in tune with certain of the most urgent tendencies and needs of modern architecture that to study them, to visit them, could have fertilized the imaginations of present-day Egyptian architects in a wonderful way if only they had been able to look at them with different eyes

(for the moment they became architects, necessarily having to learn the new construction techniques that had been imported from Europe, they went off to live in the other part of the city, they began to belong to that other part of the city, losing their normal communication with this one, ceasing to come here, at a loss to assign it a suitable place among the things they had been taught, avoiding the agitation it would have caused in them to return here),

these sublime cubes or cupolas of calm in the midst of the bazaars, and, since in Egypt Islam appeared especially as a revelation that had come from the desert, the Koran an immense voice rumbling over the desert, exquisite cool equivalents of the desert and of its silence in full valley concentration, places conceived as resonators of pure recitation.

In the South, confined inside other, even more ancient walls, whose round Roman towers served as models for that of the medieval surrounding wall, are the Coptic churches and convents associated with the memory of the hermits and their temptations.

Lastly, on the other side of the Nile, at Giza, appear the first notes of that long, inexhaustible melody that continues, for travellers going south by train, until the branching off at Fayum, the three pyramids to the base of which the tramway goes, those three immense, irrecusable monuments which, when one begins to approach them, lose the straightness of their lines, begin to resemble very large piles of stones whose size and distance one can't appreciate, so that one thinks one has already arrived when there is still quite a long way to go,

stones that increase individually in volume as one walks, assuming proportions one would not have suspected, so that a moment comes when one wonders how long this amazing growth is going to go on,

the whole then losing its shape, which is so well known, the face ahead of you now filling the entire horizon, its three points causing the eye to leap between dizzying perspectives when your hand at last touches the stone,

this tremendous response of the pharaohs to the humiliating night of the desert ("They boasted," says Bossuet, "that they were the only ones who had, like the gods, made immortal works"), a constant humiliation throughout the Middle Ages for those sultans who considered themselves the heralds of that very word thundering over the desert, a permanent scandal because of their massiveness, which rendered the process of their construction inexplicable to those who contemplated them, demanding recourse to magical powers, to the intervention of demons, the way the other ancient monuments were a permanent scandal

because of their innumerable figures, the writing itself, indecipherable, teeming with animal and human
signs,

so that if many mosques in Cairo were built with
blocks of limestone or granite that came from the pyramids, it wasn't only, as people are accustomed to sug-
gest, because of convenience, but also because of a
very directly religious necessity.

A way had to be found to affirm conclusive victory
over this prestigious past, to try to break free of this
power that had to be acknowledged and endured, as is
admirably expressed in the fact that the stone threshold of the very beautiful and very severe Khanqah of
the Sultan Bibars is an ancient stone engraved with
the cartouches of Ramses X, a very visible inscription
which one thus treads upon, that one anathematizes
every time one enters before taking off one's shoes.

Edward William Lane, the author of an admirable
book which Nerval made abundant use of, about the
customs of the Egyptians at the beginning of the 19th
century, a book which is still one of the best tools for
helping the explorer of present-day Egyptian life, declares at the beginning of his first chapter on superstitions: "It is commonly believed that the earth was
inhabited, before the time of Adam, by a race of beings
different from us in form, and much more powerful;
and that forty (or, according to some, seventy-two)
pre-adamite kings, each of whom bore the name of
Suleymán (or Salomon), successively governed this
people. The last of these Suleymáns was called Gánn

Ibn-Gánn; and from him, some think, the ginn (who are also called ganns) derive their name. Hence, some believe the ginn to be the same with the pre-adamite race here mentioned; but others assert that they (the ginn) were a distinct class of beings, and brought into subjection by the other race."

And later he says:

"The ancient tombs of Egypt, and the dark recesses of the temples, are commonly believed, by the people of this country, to be inhabited by 'efreets [that is, jinns]. I found it impossible to persuade one of my servants to enter the Great Pyramid with me, from his having this idea. Many of the Arabs ascribe the erection of the Pyramids, and all the most stupendous remains of antiquity in Egypt, to Gánn Ibn-Gánn, and his servants, the jinns; conceiving it impossible that they could have been raised by human hands."

We remember the passage in the *Voyage en Orient* in which Nerval tells us about the conversation he claims he had during a walk on the island of Roda with an old sheik whom he asked what he thought of the Pyramids, which had just come into view:

"Some authors think the Pyramids were built by the pre-adamite king Gian-ben-Gian; but, according to a tradition much more widespread among us, there existed, three hundred years before the flood, a king named Saurid, son of Salahoc, who dreamed one night that everything was turned upside down on earth, men falling on their faces . . ."

Now, this whole passage is of particular interest at this point, since we have to clarify a little how the Pyramids were viewed by Moslem Cairo in its great period, a vision that still prevails beneath the many new elements that have added to it,

since this conversation never took place the way Nerval reports it, the people talking being in reality separated by several centuries, since the words put in the mouth of the old sheik are in reality, as Jean Richer discovered, an almost literal transcription of an Arab manuscript translated by Pierre Vattier in 1666 under the title: *L'Egypte de Murtadi, fils du Gaphiphe, où il est traité des Pyramides, du débordement du Nil et des autres merveilles de cette province selon les opinions et traditions des Arabes* [the Egypt of Murtadi, son of Gaphiph, in which are discussed the Pyramids, the flooding of the Nile and the other wonders of this province according to the opinions and traditions of the Arabs], which I will now quote, going back to the original French text because it is obviously more characteristic and more illuminating for us than its adaptation:

"Then he ordered that the Pyramids be built, so that they could carry and shut up there the most precious of their treasures, with the bodies of their kings and their riches . . .

"The guard of the eastern Pyramid was an idol of black and white jamanic scale that had both eyes open and was sitting on a throne, having near it a sort of halberd, and did anyone cast his gaze upon it, he would hear a dreadful noise coming from there, that nigh made his heart fail him, and whoever heard that noise would die from it.

"The guard of the western Pyramid was an idol of

hard red stone holding in his hand likewise a sort of halberd, and having on his head a serpent twined around, which serpent struck at those who approached.

"For a guard of the third Pyramid, there was a small idol of bahe stone set on a base of the same material, which idol drew to it those who looked at it and clove to them inseparably until it made them die or made them lose their minds."

This is how he describes the contemporary phantoms that haunted them:

"They say the spirit of the southern Pyramid never appears outside save in the form of a woman naked even about her private parts, who is also beautiful . . . When she wants to give love to someone and make him lose his mind, she laughs at him and forthwith he approaches her and she draws him to her and maddens him through love so that he loses his mind then and there and runs vagabond through the country. Several people have seen her gliding around the Pyramid at noon and near sunset.

"The spirit of the second Pyramid which is the colored one, is an old Nubian man who carries a basket on his head and in his hands a censer, etc."

And again it is from Murtadi and a few other Arab historians he was able to consult in translation that Nerval borrows the details of the opening of the great Pyramid and its exploration by the caliph al-Ma'mun of the Abbasid dynasty:

"Their chronicles relate that they found in what was called the King's Room a statue of a man of black stone and a statue of a woman of white stone standing on a table, one holding a lance and the other a bow. In the middle of the table was a hermetically sealed vase which, when it was opened, was found to be full of still fresh blood. There was also a rooster of red gold speckled with hyacinths which cried out and beat its wings when one entered."

In this collection of legends, which other people, having access to original texts, could certainly study much better than I, it is not surprising that almost all the details can be precisely related to what we know today about the ancient royal Egyptian tombs since that of Tutankhamen revealed its black guards to us, its white women, its furniture, its plates and dishes, its kites and vultures of enameled gold

(in Murtadi, the discovery of the golden rooster, that Nerval, despite all his desire to believe, found a little too "thousand and one nights," is related in a somewhat more detailed way which allows us to see how its fantastic aspects were able to develop quite naturally from the discovery of some treasure in the depths of a tomb—and why not the Pyramid itself, which, if it had been despoiled from Antiquity on, certainly could have served as a hiding place once again at a relatively late date:

". . . they found a square place like a gathering place where there were many statues, among others the figure of a rooster made of red gold. This figure was fearful, speckled with hyacinths, of which there were two large ones on the two eyes, which shone like two great torches. They approached it and at once it cried out dreadfully and began to beat its two wings and at the same time they heard many voices coming to them from all sides"),

this is not surprising because of the necessary existence of a tradition of stories linked to these enduring monuments, of stories becoming more and more legendary as the relation between their various elements is less well understood, being changed according to new interpretations, but preserving a certain number of basic images revived, consolidated by the discoveries here and there of ancient objects corroborating them.

It is not at all surprising that these idols and these phantoms should have the very faces of these statues or these bas-relief figures, so troubling and so numerous,

and one can see what a prodigious depth, often expressly considered as superhuman, all this gave to the personage of the Pharaoh, Moses' interlocutor, and to the magic surrounding him in those passages in the Koran where he appears,

proclaiming in chapter xliii: "Oh my people! This kingdom of Egypt is it not mine? And these rivers which flow below me? What! Are you not able to see? Am I not superior to this contemptible creature who can hardly speak?", declaring in chapter lxxix: "I am your Lord God Almighty,"

what illumination all this gave to that pride, what an explanation, an explanation that would really have become too good, in contradiction to the sacred text, if one had made him out directly to have been the builder of the Pyramids, if one had identified with one of them the tower whose plan is attributed to him by the Koran:

"Oh you leaders! I know of no other gods for you besides me; therefore, have clay baked, Oh Haman, and build me a tower, so that I may climb up to that so-called God of Moses; for, in truth, I think he is a liar!"

and this is why he was considered solely, in conformance with the historic truth, as the distant heir of their builders, which already introduced into that obscure and as if faltering reference to Antiquity, a great internal dislocation, the idea of a great distance between certain of its moments, consequently the idea of an historical duration much longer than that marked by the three great reference points enumerated in the Koran, the three points of origin of the three religions currently present, Moses, Jesus, Mohammed, whence the notion of "before the Flood," or "before Adam," which plays exactly the same role.

Thus the use, as quarry, of these ancient monuments so terribly there, so terribly near (and that was the immense difference between Egypt and other countries of the Middle East where the vestiges of remote Antiquity, which were completely covered with sand, which only came back to light after excavation, did not directly trouble the Moslem Middle Ages at all),

the re-use of these stones is a response to their superstitious power, to the persistence, accursed for the conqueror, of habits and beliefs linked to them;

but the result of this response, since the destruction of the ancient monument remains insignificant, changes almost nothing about its imposing mass, since the presence of these ancient stones in the new monuments is evident from the exoticism of their material, granite of Asswan, for example, and far from obliterating that power and that endurance, preserves it, stabilizes it, accentuates it.

What is more, as it is only when the old attitude is obviously in contradiction to the new order that it takes on this status of witchcraft, and that other aspects of it come to be integrated quite naturally into the teaching of the conqueror, into his way of life, come to give him little by little, subtly, smoothly, an altogether original physiognomy compared to the one he had before and to the one he has taken on in other landscapes against backgrounds less encumbered, less rich,

color him even in his most official manifestations,

the use of these artificial quarries is in some sense the material corollary of that contamination, and therefore the very configuration of Moslem Cairo; its difference in structure, compared to other great cities of Islam, illustrates the particularities of Egyptian Islam, the singular characteristics of the historic and geographical soil on which it developed,

which manifests itself with great clarity in a feature of the city of Cairo which I haven't yet mentioned, that is, the extent and magnificence of its necropolises, unlike Istanbul, for example, with its fields of steles packed together in the shadow of a sanctuary or unfurled over the surrounding hills as though tossed by the wind, here we have neighborhoods for the dead more or less similar to those of the living, with a more or less equal area, only still more dilapidated, with their streets and their squares, with their funerary mosques, the tombs of the sultans, as sumptuous, as lofty as those other mosques in the interior, which often contain tombs as well,

including here and there, at the main crossroads, veritable small villages of shops among the mausoleums, for welcoming the inhabitants of the other streets, the other squares, because of the size and frequency of the funeral ceremonies, not only of the burials but also of those long visits paid to the dead on the occasion of certain holidays, during which people come to eat, chat, sleep next to the tombs,

which for the wealthy used to include a true underground chamber so that "the person or persons buried in it," as Lane says, "may be able with ease to sit up when visited and examined by the two angels, Munkar and Nekee,"

a private judgment in preparation for which an "instructor of the dead" would lecture him at the time of the closing of the tomb (just as in the ancient tombs the cadaver was, if possible, provided with passages from the *Book of the Dead*, that famous negative confession that was supposed to help one pass the test victoriously), declaring to him (I am still quoting Lane):

131

"O servant of God! O son of a handmaid of God! know that, at this time, there will come down to thee two angels commissioned respecting thee and the like of thee: when they say to thee: 'Who is thy Lord?' answer them, 'God is my Lord,' in truth; and when they ask thee concerning thy Prophet, or the man who hath been sent unto you, say to them, 'Mohammad is the Apostle of God,' with veracity; and when they ask thee concerning thy religion, say to them, 'El-Islám is my religion;' and when they ask thee concerning thy book of direction, say to them, 'The Kur-án is my book of direction, and the Muslims are my brothers;' and when they ask thee concerning thy Kibleh, say to them, 'The Kaabeh is my Kibleh and I have lived and died in the assertion that there is no deity but God, and Mohammad is God's Apostle;' and they will say, 'Sleep, O servant of God, in the protection of God.'"

This attention paid to death, this familiarity with the cadaver, whose smell on the warmest days impregnates the whole Valley, this constant awareness of the transitory nature of the individual, so different from the sort of obliviousness towards that condition that exists now in most countries of Western Europe, so that when someone dies, it always seems to be an unexpected event, we don't know how to behave, how to talk, how to get rid of the scandalous body,

that enormous importance accorded to the tomb is very closely connected to the structure of the Valley's landscape, to that very clear humiliation of the transitory human and his domain by another, permanent

world, and it is consequently necessary that in its response to such a situation, every civilization that has
come from somewhere else, come from a region in
which the question of the dead body was posed with
much less violence, so that it was possible to hide it, to
more or less neglect it—that it adopt the solutions, the
customs of those that preceded it here.

The civilization of Moslem Egypt was therefore
made up of a balance between elements whose age and
whose origins were very different; now, what the European presence brings about is not only the destruction,
around certain objects, certain persons, certain new
teachings, of old habits which taken together formed a
coherent way of life and thought that it doesn't succeed in replacing in a satisfactory way,

it is also the dissociation of those elements that
were formerly in balance, so that the constitution, the
invention of a new balance becomes an even more
difficult problem that cannot be resolved until the historical relations of all these present domains are clari-
fied.

In fact, the European infiltration will not fail to affect
these ancient monuments, with which so many ways of
doing and thinking have been bound up; far from par-
ticipating, like earlier waves of civilizations, in demol-
ishing them, obliterating them, burying them in a
thicker dust and darkness, it is going to increase their
presence through its archaeologists, exhume them, restore them, explore them and study them, exalt them,
project onto them and onto the whole world to which

they testify a completely new light, completely different from the ambiguous glimmer that used to mark them;

through the development of a tourism that focuses primarily upon them, it is going to make them play a quite unexpected role in the economy of the country, thus recalling them constantly to the attention of the Egyptian even if he doesn't live near them, in a way that wasn't foreseen, the whole former attitude towards them therefore requiring a complete revision.

In France or in other Western countries there are certainly scholars who are studying Islam, who probably are more familiar with certain aspects of its history or its literature than the professors at El Azhar, who are capable of providing much better editions of certain texts, others who are studying Ancient Egypt or Coptic Christianity, but, in the Valley of the Nile, what is at once so dramatic and so exciting is that each farmer, no matter how uncultivated, how deprived he may be, finds himself daily faced with the question of the respective situation of these worlds in relation to one another and in relation to modern Europe, or America, whose technology, whose thought is submerging him,

a question he is obviously incapable of answering for the moment, which he can leave tranquilly in suspense so long as he is still far enough away from a factory or a school, but which will eventually gnaw at him and cloud his mind, to the point where it will prevent him from learning correctly what he might want and need to know once he sets about it.

Now, what can be called average European thinking,

that is, the mental structure common to those French or English or American merchants, engineers, professors who held so much power, the thinking which at that time wholly inspired their modern universities (I am speaking of 1950–1951, before Farouk left), could not really help the Egyptians in this respect, and still can't.

For, if it demands a historical perspective of a certain type, the one it has to offer is inadequate in its temporal and geographical dimensions.

In effect, every Frenchman, for example, especially if he has had secondary schooling, is able to give a rough summary of the history of mankind in which will figure the Greeks, the Romans (also the Jews, to whom we owe the Bible and the Catholic religion, but that is a special area, which people often prefer not to bring up), then the Christian Middle Ages, the Renaissance, and finally modern Europe, with its science, which conquers the rest of the world,

a schema which seems sufficient, allowing as it does for all the explanations without having to bring in those other nations, those other civilizations, the strange, curious, exotic, amusing ones, to which a serious, well-balanced person, a gentleman concerned with business or politics would think it rather silly to pay any real attention,

so that entities as enormous and prestigious as Ancient Egypt and Islam only appear in their representation of the universe as appendices, footnotes, half-humorous vignettes,

as little secondary regions whose existence can very

well be ignored since, in principle, that existence doesn't change anything, explain anything,

and whose works and language certain eccentrics clearly have a right to study if they have enough leisure time for that,

to explore the ruins, if they bring back statues or jewels to enrich the museums or collections, which is a flattering luxury for everyone, but which one is quite ready to consider as unreasonable, to strike from the list of expenses.

Naturally this schema can be of no use at all to even the humblest Egyptian peasant, since within his perspective it is primarily pharaonic antiquity that constitutes a riddle, it is primarily Islam that constitutes a past or tradition, so that he finds himself having to situate European history, history such as it is reflected by one of those Europeans he may meet in the streets of Cairo or in the hotels of Luxor, within a much vaster context,

an enormous task, a monstrous task, but so urgent that a start will certainly be made upon it soon and a new way of looking at and interpreting history will be invented, will spread through this country, as in all the great countries of the East in upheaval, a way of interpreting history that will necessarily react upon that of Europe itself, bringing with it immense changes of emphasis and outlook,

a task which I myself was faced with, living in that country, finding that I had in some sense become one of them, one who had especially forgotten his origins and who had particularly well assimilated what Europe teaches, as though I had been born in that country, had left it for France when I was very small, and coming here had really come back,

if I wanted to survive intact, if I wanted to remain open-eyed, if I wanted to escape that ruin, that intellectual desolation overcoming my colleagues at the Minya lycée, who were so much less, so scandalously less favored than I.

Also, just as thenceforth my visits to Cairo were no longer mere returns to a Europe I missed, but the most potent tool I could have for analyzing modern Egypt, for seeing it better, in the same way, very soon, visiting an ancient site was no longer a simple matter of esthetic escapism; it was tied to an effort to rethink, to enlarge the perspectives I had inherited from my education, an effort the need for which I had clearly felt already before I left France, but only distantly, disinterestedly, certainly not with this precision, this urgency, this acuteness.

Thus the amazing Djéser monument at Saqqara, for example, as it had been rediscovered and restored, such a new puzzle for the inhabitants of Egypt, became a consuming puzzle for me too, and no longer merely an object which one admires and at which one looks with an astonished but detached gaze; it became so bound to me that a certain region of my consciousness could only become clear to the extent that I could better understand, better picture to myself the reasons why those men of five thousand years ago, in such a violent explosion of inventive genius, built with such care those false doors, those delicate houses filled with rough boulders, that stepped Pyramid which only emerged from the sand a few years ago, and what relation all that has to what came after it;

thus, in the tomb of Petosiris at Tounah el-Jebel, near Minya, from the Persian period, on the walls of which, I knew, were engraved maxims certain of which had been translated literally in the *Book of Proverbs*, what I was looking for was some illumination of my origins and of that of the religion in which I had been brought up and was looking for this perhaps even more clearly still in the sterilized amphitheater of El-Amarna,

a renewal, an improvement in the position of problems that had troubled me for years and were troubling me there much more directly and profoundly.

Not being an Egyptologist at all, I must be content with simply pointing to this area; I would like to do no more than show what a source of illumination there may be in this gigantic nest of problems which the researchers' scrupulously careful picks are unearthing, causing to hum like a swarm of wasps, as they study them and solve them,

not only for understanding this contemporary country which slyly keeps referring back to itself, but for Europe itself, daughter of the Roman Empire, within which a quantity of scattered signals keep pointing to that hearth whose radiance is almost as ambiguous for us as it is for the Moslems of Cairo.

Now the place where this hearth opens up most perfectly, spreads out, and proffers itself, splendid to examine, whatever the beauties of the other sites may be,
is obviously that enormous city of tombs and temples
on the two banks at Luxor, certainly the most impressive known group of ruins, ancient Thebes which
even in its worst abandonment has never ceased to
emit a constant, secret glow—to which I would ask for
no other testimony than the description of it in Bossuet:

"In the Said (as you know, this is the name for the
Thebaid) they have discovered temples and palaces
still almost intact, where those columns and statues are
innumerable. Here one admires above all a palace
whose remains seem to have survived only in order to
outshine the glory of all the greatest works. Four alleys
as far as the eye can see, delimited on either side by
sphinxes of a substance as rare as they are striking in
size, serve as an avenue leading to four porticoes
whose height astonishes one's eyes. What magnificence and what scale! Those who have described this
amazing structure to us have not had time to go all
around it, and are not even sure they have seen half of
it; but everything they saw was astounding. One hall,
which was apparently the middle of this superb palace,
was supported by six score columns six men's arms
around, proportionately high, and intermingled with
obelisks still upright despite the passing of so many
centuries. Even the colors, that is, the soonest to feel
the power of time, yet endure among the ruins of that

admirable structure, and preserve their brightness, such was the ability of Egypt to imprint the character of immortality upon all her works."

This is in the third part of the *discours,* and of course one starts imagining the other direction classical French art could have taken, the other face Versailles might have shown us, had the advice he gives in the following paragraph ever been followed:

"Now that the name of the King is reaching the most unknown parts of the world, and now that this prince is sending so far for the finest works of nature and art, would it not be a fit object of that noble curiosity, to uncover the beauties which the Thebaid contains in its wilderness, and to enrich our architecture with the inventions of Egypt? What power and what art were able to make of such a country the wonder of the world?"

Now he realized that Imperial Rome, on whose memory Imperial France was endeavoring from a distance to model itself, was even more sensitive to Egypt's prestige, which he himself experienced so strongly through the intermediary of a traveller's description, for Bossuet went on to say:

"It was left to Egypt alone to raise monuments for posterity. Its obelisks are still the principal ornament of Rome today, as much because of their beauty as because of their loftiness; and the power in Rome, despairing of equalling the Egyptians, felt it had done enough for its grandeur when it borrowed their kings' monuments."

And to mark clearly to what extent our knowledge of Egyptian antiquity is still in its infancy, not only because of the dim inheritance made up of countless prejudices towards it and which can only be got rid of slowly, but also because of the bulk of the documentary material itself that has to be deciphered and sorted out, it is enough to say that when I went to Luxor for the first time, in February, during the mid-year vacation, one of the young Egyptologists I met there told me that in his free time he was recopying the inscriptions that completely covered the walls of that part of the temple at Karnak which is famous and has been for so long, that great hypostyle hall where, as Bossuet says, a few colors "yet endure" but much less well, with much less freshness than in certain other monuments that have been unearthed since, for example in the wonderful temple of Seti I at Abydos,

he was collating these inscriptions, which had never been done before because these were only ritual texts and the most urgent thing was naturally for the scholars to recopy, publish and interpret everything that allows dates to be established.

I returned to Luxor in May, since my French colleagues from Minya and I were giving exams in Qena, the neighboring prefecture. The time of very great heat had already arrived; not a single tourist was left; we had it all to ourselves.

One morning, at five o'clock, we took the boat we had rented the night before, steered by a boy of thirteen or fourteen to whose father we had paid five piastres, fifty francs in all, for the entire day, and we went to the bank of the dead.

This time, to get into the long winding ravine among

the dazzling rocks that ends at the Valley of the Kings, we chose not to go by way of that cirque that has dug itself in the mountain in the shape of a pyramid,

that mountain which was interpreted as a natural pyramid, centuries and centuries after the first ones had been raised by men,

this funerary monument built by the gods for the sovereigns who were their brothers, as people had known for a long time then, and who endeavored to make sure people remembered it by erecting their succession of funerary temples down below, facing the river,

we didn't take those strange black barouches pulled by thin horses, long lines of which had been collected by the tourist organizations for their groups,

but we found a donkey-driver who accompanied us throughout our long tour.

We saw a few of the royal sepulchers that are the hardest to get to, notably that of Thutmose III with its great oval hall where, with his acetylene lamp, the guardian illuminated for us the walls along whose length ran so effectively schematized illustrations of the book of what is in Hades,

then we visited a few of the hundred other numbered tombs, we went onto the terraces of Deir el-Bahari, we must have lunched at the "resthouse" near the Ramesseum on the provisions we had brought along, fallen asleep . . .

I no longer remember the order very well, it has all become a little confused, things have become something of a jumble . . .

But in the evening a scene took place that summed up for me my whole Egyptian itinerary, in which were symbolically resolved all the swarm of difficulties I had raised with every new step and which was in some sense Egypt's answer, in some sense its fundamental acquiescence to the very lively interrogation I had begun to address to it.

As we had just left the necropolis of Deir el-Medina, on the path, a tall Egyptian peasant, wearing a very neat, long, dark blue, almost black robe and a little white turban, stopped us, greeted us, me especially, with an air of great joy.

I understood absolutely nothing of what he said to me, what he wanted of me, the reason for his attitude, when suddenly among his words I recognized these four syllables: *André Lebon.*

It was the name of the ship I had taken at Marseilles seven months earlier, with another friend who wasn't there, who had ended up in a different Egyptian city from mine, a ship that did not usually do the Alexandria run, but was that one time replacing the *Champollion,* which was being repaired,

a ship whose hold had been fitted out to transport troops to Indochina, hammocks slung one above another all around the great square hatch reached by a long ladder, covered with a big tarpaulin at night and when it rained,

and this time accommodated steerage passengers, including us.

When we left, each of us had been given an old metal plate, flatware, and a mug, which we would carefully stow away so that we could find them again at the next meal, and which we didn't always find, so that we would appropriate others that were lying around here and there,

passengers who were not entitled to service, so that two of us, we were told, would either have to volunteer or be picked to go to the galley and get bread, wine, mess-tins of soup and other food (it was always my friend and I, as soon as the hour sounded, because we were absolutely determined to have hot food), which we balanced as we climbed down the steps of the ladder, but often on windy days, not skilfully enough to prevent food from spilling over, making star-shaped puddles on the table below.

For four days we lived this way, in this sort of primitive state, surrounded by vomit, in this sort of commoners' locker, in this pit from the edges of which ladies would sometimes gaze down, my philosopher friend and I, as well as a young Lebanese who had just finished his hitch in the Foreign Legion and was going to set himself up as a hairdresser in Beirut, some rich students from Cairo who had spent their vacations in Paris, where they had run through a little too much money, various individuals of dubious professions, the Egyptian gymnastics team, except for their star, who, having picked up a medal, qualified for a first class ticket, coming back from some championship or other,

who had all given a demonstration of their talents before the whole ship, the captain presiding, a pleasant interlude being provided by a contortionist who was also a beauty king, Mr. Egypt or something like that, and who was also coming back from a meet along with his wife, the only woman in that hold,

and in a bunk not far from mine (there were many empty ones, but only some of the lamps worked), smiling, a peasant from Upper Egypt who didn't know a word of French, the only one who was not wearing European clothes, but was dressed in a very neat, long, blue, almost black robe, on his head a felt skullcap surrounded by a very clean white turban, and that, so we managed to understand, because he was the servant of a man who worked at Luxor and who had taken him along with him to Paris during his summer vacation, a man who was himself returning second class, upstairs, with his wife and children,

to Paris which had amazed him and from where he had brought back in his suitcase a talisman he would only show, with extreme caution, to people he thought would be just as enchanted by it as he was:

a stereoscope with about ten views: the Opéra, the Arc de Triomphe, etc.,

this peasant, whom I at last recognized on the path near the cemetery of Deir el-Medina, the excavating of which was overseen by his employer, absent for the moment.

We got off our donkeys; we went into the little village, into his earth house, into his room furnished only with an extravagant large brass bed, surely brought to Luxor decades ago for one of the big hotels on the other bank.

145

Then, we having finished drinking the burning hot mint tea brought by one of those women who laugh in the window recesses, he went to get the stereoscope, which for me, too, in the meantime, had become a talisman.

And so, after a whole day's gorging on sunlight and Antiquity, in the cool shade of this room, thanks to the friendship of this man with whom we couldn't really talk, whom I wouldn't have imagined seeing again, whom I certainly wouldn't have recognized if he hadn't recognized me first,

we were able to contemplate, delighted, more surprised and more overwhelmed even than we had been on the day of the one true rainfall at Minya,

those streets which had been so familiar to us, but which had become so remote to us during our stay, the Champs-Elysées and especially the Place de la Concorde, with its obelisk in the middle; and though we had been aware before, though we had certainly heard it said, that this was an obelisk from Luxor, it was only now that we began to grasp the meaning and the implications of the phrase.

And I knew very well that for the understanding that existed between us, which was so secure and so pure but which remained mute, to pass to the level of language, for it to be able to develop into a real conversation, there would have had to be an already existing organization at the level of this language, one to which we could have referred, on which we could have relied,

an organization, satisfactory to both of us, of those

various places and times that were contracted into the present moment.

We stayed for a long time drinking in the coolness that flowed from those pictures, then one of my friends reminded us that we had told our boatman that we would be back before sundown.

Now the sun was already very low, and was sinking more and more rapidly.

We got back up on our donkeys, casting long shadows before us through the red air, like the pylons of the funeral temple of Ramses III to our right, like the colossi of Memnon to our left, and I felt extraordinarily happy because, yes, something of the world had been unveiled for me, in a confused way, but in an absolute certainty that would never leave me, the slight pain I felt between my vertebrae, the fatigue that suddenly overwhelmed me, being in some sense the guarantee of it.

The night had long since fallen when we reached the riverbank. Our boatman complained.

When will I return to Egypt?